In the School of Love

By:
Fr. Slavko Barbarić, O.F.M.

Translated by:
The Sarcevic Family

Published by:
Faith Publishing Company
P.O. Box 237
Milford, OH 45150

D1617151

Publisher herein recognizes that the final authority regarding the validity of claimed apparitions rests with the Holy See of Rome to whose judgment we willingly submit.

Published in the U.S.A. by:
Faith Publishing Company
P.O. Box 237
Milford, Ohio 45150

Originally published in Medjugorje, Bosnia-Hercegovina as:
U Sole Ljube
1993, Zupini Ured, Medjugorje

English Translation from the Croatian by The Sarcevic Family

Cover: Photograph of flowers from the shrine to Our Lady, Queen of Peace, in front of St. James Church, Medjugorje.

ISBN: 1-880033-18-6

Library of Congress Card No.: 95-060456

CONTENTS

Love is not a gift given only to the good,
but a fundamental condition of life for all!

FOREWORD

One more spiritual booklet from Father Slavko Barbarić! *In the School of Love* is a small book, but it contains a wealth of shining jewels which disperse darkness and illuminate horizons for the human, temporal voyage toward the "harbor of salvation."

Father Slavko's earlier books dealt with the stem and core of the Christian and divine life. This booklet is a direct spark from the original source, the Divine. That source and origin is **love:** love which is a definition of God's name and His meaning; a definition of the name of Jesus and His meaning; a love which moved God Himself to become man and, for the sake of man, to die on the Cross. It is the all-encompassing and awesome divine love with which the man of God loves God above all and loves his neighbors as himself. From the divine, endless spring and from the divine, limitless ocean comes this spiritual booklet. However, for quite obvious reasons, this booklet has its spiritual epicenter and spark in the more than thirteen years of spiritual happenings and movements on the holy ground of the Queen of Peace in Medjugorje.

Father Slavko begins each chapter of this booklet with a message from Our Lady; messages received through the visionary Marija Pavlović. The pure and original, divine love to which Our Lady constantly and tirelessly encourages us is ingrained in the stem of each of these messages. Following each, Father Slavko gives a short teaching. These teachings are based upon and empowered by the unassailable and timeless divine teaching. At the end of each chapter Father Slavko has included a suitable passage from Scripture which recaps and confirms all that he has said. As a result, this spiritual reading appears as a condensation of material powerfully woven from the words of Our Lady and Our Lord, with the author's insightful words of encouragement and motivations; or as a three part harmonious braid interlacing all that the life of a faithful Christian and the life of Our Lord makes inseparable. One thing can definitely be guaranteed. Whoever reads this booklet most certainly will not be bored. The one who reads it attentively will become richer by a few of its jewels.

—Jakov Bubalo, O.F.M.

INTRODUCTION

Dear Reader:

Take this booklet and read it. It was compiled with love. My purpose in writing this book is to witness to the love of the Mother; a Mother who speaks and who loves. In speaking with love, this Mother creates a disposition to listen in the hearts of her own. Read and listen to what she says. Her messages are the first words which you will find on the following pages. She speaks with love and about love. She always begins with the motherly words: *Dear Children!* Meditate with me on her guidance. Then, read a thought chosen from the inexhaustible richness of the Divine Word which is offered as spiritual food, heavenly bread for our life, for our healing and for our salvation. Her words which are tender, dear, encouraging, determined, and sometimes reprimanding are an expression of her love for each one of us. She wants to make us completely hers, and that means to make us people of faith, hope, and love. She wants to help us pull ourselves out of the mud of this earth and rise towards the heights of vivifying love and unceasing beauty. The reality is that our face is disfigured, our heart is wounded, our families are destroyed, our air contaminated and our friendships shaken. It is hard for us. At each step there is the threat of death; love cooled off. Our Mother is giving us a promise that through love we will become beautiful. Disfigurement will disappear and there will be no more death. But this can happen only through love!

Decide now to be a diligent student of this *school of love*. Raise your eyes and let the Divine beauty overwhelm you, and you will travel more easily through this valley of death towards the dawn of life!

HERE IS YOUR MOTHER

To be in a school where love is taught means to be in the most beautiful school. Whoever is with the Mother is in the school of love and whoever wants to be in the school of love, unconditionally has to be with the Mother.

In Medjugorje, the visionaries, the parish community of Medjugorje, pilgrims from all over the world, prayer groups, communities, individuals, and the whole church have been with the Mother of Christ, the Mother of the Church, for more than twelve years. And being the Mother of all mothers, of all fathers, of all children, with the Mother of all people, they are truly in the school of love!

So, in Medjugorje we all are in the school of love with the Mother who accepted all of us when, through her faithful love, she partook in the death of her Son with love. While her Son was dying on the Cross, with her heart pierced with pain, she heard the words, "Mother, here is your son." In this testament of a son who was ending His earthly life, all human sons have been included until the end of the world. Accepting the death of her only Son, which He offered for the salvation of the world, the Mother was not left without a Son, but rather, with love, she opened her heart to all human children and became the Mother of us all! The death of her Son did not destroy life, nor sonship, nor motherhood, but rather it enlarged them without limits!

At the moment of death only *love* can give birth to life. Only *love* can transform the moments of sadness to joy, transience into serenity, and loneliness into communion with a multitude.

Everything is possible with love. Love transforms the temporal into eternity, turns everything to good and recognizes in every person a person it can love.

To live with this Mother, to be consecrated to her, to be

1

open and devoted to her, and at the same time, to be her student is a great gift and grace. Mary, the Mother and the teacher of Christ, wants to be our Mother and teacher. She was the first one to be nourished from the spring of divine love when she became the Mother of Love. With love she wants to lead each of her children to that same spring of Love. And, that is the condition for life. As our material existence depends on our relation with the sun, so our material and spiritual existence depend on our relation with eternal love. In the event of a complete break from all connection with the sun, whatever exists would turn into darkness, ice, and eternal death. By the same token, by walking away from the spring of Love, the world is threatened with total destruction. Mary is Mother of love and life. She knows the way and the conditions. She is present and active and she wants to lead all to life!

* * * * * * *

"WHY ARE YOU SO BEAUTIFUL?"

Overwhelmed by the beauty of the Mother whom she was allowed to experience, Jelena Vasilj, a girl from the village who experiences mystical inner voices, asked the question which every child would ask her mother, "Gospa (Our Lady), why are you so beautiful?"

With the hint of a smile, Our Lady answered, *I am beautiful because I love you. If you wish to be beautiful, love.*

The human heart, without exception, yearns for beauty. Beauty makes it happy, more peaceful, and fulfilled. It makes it better and brings it to the fullness of life. Beauty helps to build the human heart, just as ugliness can destroy it. The heart yearns for beauty.

This is a major reason why the world is tireless in its search for beauty. Certainly this is not the case of external beauty only, but it is about something much deeper. This is the case for beauty which manifests itself in love, the love of a mother, father, a sister, of children, and of friends. It is the case also about the beauty of human relations, about the beauty of togetherness and about the beauty of creatures and human creation.

Let us recall that in a mother's love no child is ugly and should not be cast aside. But all children are beautiful. And every child looks at his mother as being most beautiful. And it is the truth. Because to every mother a child is someone most beautiful and so every human creature is beautiful, because it is a child even when it grows up. Therefore all people are beautiful and worthy of love! So, we are beautiful within ourselves and so are others!

But because of this reality questions arise: Why are there so many unhappy people and why are there so many conditions for our accepting others, when it is already clear that we should be beautiful to one another and happy with each other?

The answer is in our relation and desire for love. Neither age, nor sickness, nor anything in this world can endanger our beauty. We are beautiful because we are the loved children of our most beautiful Mother. To the extent that others will become more and more beautiful to us every day, and we to them, our love grows and matures.

*   *   *   *   *   *   *

IF YOU WOULD ONLY KNOW. . .

To be loved and to be able to love means to discover the purpose and joy of life independent of all life's circumstances. The life of the person who is loved is filled with purpose. And the one who loves realizes life in its fullness. The greater the love, the more giving, the more trusting a person is and the easier and more beautiful life becomes.

The visionaries gave us the following words of Our Lady, *Dear children, if you would only know how much I love you, you would leap for joy!*

The deep recognition that we are loved and that we love is tied in with everything we experience and how we experience it. Today's man is often tired. He is tired not only physically, but he is bored with life. There is no greater hardship than the boredom suffered by a person who is tired of life. This kind of fatigue is deeply connected with a lack of love toward others and a lack of security of the love of others toward us. Every person desires to overcome the fatigue which makes us tired. However, there are cases when a person is so tired of life that he doesn't even want rest. Then the disconnection of life takes place. What does this mean?

The deepest rest is to be found in love and, with love, all fatigue is overcome. All life's burdens and crosses become light. With love, it is easy to live and easy to die. Neither health nor sickness can endanger the one who loves and who knows that he is loved. When the soul is restful in love, success does not create conceit, and failure does not bring despair. Therefore, remember that you are loved so much by the Mother that your heart can leap with joy now. Remember that the Mother loves you and life's fatigue will disappear and you will take joy in everything created and in every human being.

The Mother's love is given to you unconditionally. It does not request anything from you except that you let yourself be loved. Do not allow yourself to be tired because of limited and conditional human love, but rather leap and sing from joy because of Our Lady's love. Her love does not wait for you to become good in order for her to love you, but she loves you so that you can become better and continue to grow to the fullness for which your heart yearns.

With the exception of a mother, people usually wait for you to be the way they want you to be in order to love you. That is not the case here. As soon as you open yourself to her love, people around you will be happy, joyful, peaceful and able to cope with life.

Pray that you can witness her love to every person, so that everyone will leap for joy because you love that person. We have enough reason and help to do this because God is sending a message to us through Mary, *If you only knew how much I love you, you would leap for joy!*

*　　*　　*　　*　　*　　*　　*

THE MOST BEAUTIFUL and the HARDEST MESSAGE

During an apparition, the visionary, Marija Pavlović Lunetti, asked Our Lady, "Gospa (Our Lady), do you have something especially for me?" The answer was, *I am giving you my love, so that you can give it to others.*

On one occasion I asked Marija if she could single out the one message that was the most beautiful and the hardest. After a short pause she remembered the above question and Our Lady's answer. I wanted to know why this was the most beautiful and the hardest message. She answered, "To experience the beauty of Our Lady's love and to realize that this love is a gift, is something most beautiful in life. But when I try to love others and to give this love to others, it is so hard that often I am ashamed of my incomplete love in the light of Our Lady's all-encompassing, motherly love."

Then, "What can be done?" I asked once more.

The visionary answered, "Well, I pray every day that I can be open more and more to the love of Our Lady and that I can hand it over to everyone. I pray for others that they will be able to experience this love and transmit it to others. We are so far from love toward one another and that is a sign that we are far from God's love. The closer we would come to God's love, the easier our life and our witnessing to others would be."

I believe that there is no better way for the rest of us, than daily prayer for the gift of love, so that we can experience that love which is most beautiful and accomplish what is the hardest.

*   *   *   *   *   *   *

AN EXPERIENCE of HELPLESSNESS

During the period from March 1984 to January 1987, Our Lady gave a message every Thursday through visionary Marija Pavlović. Since January 25, 1987, she gives a message only once a month. Our Lady announced this change, but she did not explain it.

Often people ask how the visionary receives messages and how does she pass them on to others. Marija explains that her receiving the message is not like a telephone call, nor is it a dictation like in school, but rather it is a deep impression which the visionary translates. On the other hand, all the visionaries have the experience that Our Lady speaks in the Croatian language. In order to feel the weight of the question and answer, I will use an example which can help us.

On the 21st day of August, 1986, Our Lady gave the following message: *Dear Children! I am thanking you for the love which you are showing to me. You know, dear children, that I love you immeasurably and day in and day out I pray to the Lord to help you so that you would understand the love which I am expressing to you. Therefore, dear children, pray, pray, pray! Thank you for having responded to my call.*

After writing the message, the visionary gave me the paper on which she had written it. At the same time she cried saying, "This is not a good message! I will tell Our Lady not to give messages through me any more!" I was uncomfortable. I took the paper and read the written words and immediately tried to convince her that the message was beautiful and that she wrote the message without any grammatical mistakes. However, Marija was not convinced and continued to cry. We talked later and I understood to a degree what her concern was.

When the visionary "heard" the words, "I love you immeasurably," it was not an ordinary word, but rather it was an experience of the reality of immeasurable love. However, when she wrote the message and held in her hand just a dead paper with lifeless letters, she felt in her heart a great disparity and she accused herself of a great betrayal. The reality of an immeasurable love and the encounter with it produced a deep joy and awakened in her heart a desire to transfer this same experience to others. But these facts manifested themselves in the heart of the visionary as two distinct and unreachable realities. For her, there was nothing else left at that moment but to cry bitterly.

Love, in its own way, relies on love and invites us to trust, to truth, and to mercy. If there is no natural response to such love talk, it causes pain in the heart, crying, sadness, and anxiety. The divine kiss of the divine love desires to pull us forward.

* * * * * * *

CORRECT DIAGNOSIS

While I was preparing this book and thinking about the messages and the guidance which our Mother and Teacher is giving us, I understood something and, for a moment I was awestruck. Then I became frightened, but in the end, consoled. It is easy for all of us to judge ourselves or others saying, "I'm nervous, angry," or "He's unapproachable, closed," "She's impatient, sensitive, irritable, distracted," "He has no time," "I'm tired." I understood that in these situations we forget that the reason for these stages most often is the absence of love. Because when I love someone, then I have time and I am attentive, smiling, and compassionate. While, however, if I do not love, the signs of impatience and mistrust appear, and I tend to say the other has no patience!

This is a wrong diagnosis and because of the wrong diagnosis the wrong means of healing are applied and a person really begins to suffer. If we understood that this is a question of the absence of love, we would more easily find the key for the solution. And the key is called *love*.

When I love I have time, I have patience, I am attentive and I am vulnerable. But when I do not love, then I lose my temper and I do not have time and things make me tired and angry. Therefore, the state of love is, at the same time, a way to peace, to understanding and to forgiveness. A state of no-love is the path to destruction. We can preserve our inner peace and remain rested only if we love. We live in a constant rat race. If people loved many would be saved from psychological illnesses, and in a great part, from many physical illnesses. The way of love is the way of life!

* * * * * * *

CHOSEN and GUARDED in LOVE

Dear Children! I have chosen this parish in a special way and I wish to lead it. I am guarding it in love and I want everyone to be mine. Thank you for having responded tonight. I wish you always to be with me and my Son in ever greater numbers. I shall speak a message to you every Thursday (March 1, 1984).

To love means to be open to an individual, to all beings, to all creatures, to God. The more we love, the more open we become and the more we encompass all beings. Conditions, boundaries, strangers, outsiders, the outcasts—these are all signs of captivity, signs of limited love. Divine love knows none of these limitations. It encompasses all people and all that is created, because everything is created from love. With this in mind, it is obvious that all of us are chosen by God's love. God decided for us unconditionally. Love does not want to lose anyone. Therefore, it tries to guard all and save all. Love opposes loss, destruction and disappearance. Divine love, therefore, possessively guards its loved ones. God, Himself, is possessive because He guards everything with love. And the loss of anyone affects Him. He suffers.

Mary chooses a parish community and guards it. By choosing a parish community, she once more confirms the choosing of each individual. The parish community by itself is the Church and at the same time part of the greater Church. Other parish communities, however, should not be jealous, but should joyfully participate in the fact of choosing. The choice of this parish community only confirms and clarifies to people from all parish communities that they too are chosen and that they are not forgotten. Mary wants to guard and gather her own. She wants all to be present, not to go astray and not to be lost. Love creates and wants togetherness. Mary, therefore, desires that we gather in greater numbers.

The joy with which the parish community participates is the response to the given love. One who knows that he is loved, wishes to become like the one who loves him and tries to do everything to respond with love. Numerous pilgrims confirm that they regard this parish community as their own and return to stay in it with joy. It is a sign of gifted consciousness that God, through Mary, loves, guards and gathers His own.

May the God and Father of Our Lord Jesus Christ be praised. He has blessed us with every spiritual blessing in the Heavens through Christ. God chose us through Him before the world began, to be holy and without blemish before Him, to be full of love; He predestined us to be His sons through Jesus Christ, by the decision of His will for the praise and glory of His mercy (Eph. 1:3-6).

*　*　*　*　*　*　*

LOVE EDUCATES

Dear Children! Thank you for dedicating all your hard work to God even now when He is testing you through the grapes you are picking. Be assured, dear children, that He loves you and, therefore, He tests you. Always offer up all your burdens to God and do not be anxious. Thank you for having responded to my call (October 11, 1984).

The prayer group that gathers around the visionary Ivan meets for prayer usually out in the open. They go to the Hill of Apparition or to Cross Mountain and they gather normally in the evening hours from nine o'clock on. They even have had prayer meetings after midnight. Our Lady invites them to pray at different times of the day and in all weather conditions, in summer and winter, in the rain and in the cold. During the prayer meeting Our Lady appears to Ivan and to other visionaries, if they are present.

One cold, windy evening I asked Ivan why Our Lady invited them to Cross Mountain that night when it was so cold. How can the one whom they call a caring mother invite them to go out so late and during cold weather, when every reason says that it would be better to stay at home. My question did not confuse the visionary but he wondered that I would question it. He answered, "One who loves you and cares about you, should also have the courage to ask something from you!"

Neither the prayer group nor the visionaries ask such questions, but rather, go and do that which is asked of them.

After this answer, I remained speechless. I said, "Well, if this is so, then, good luck!" I understood, however, the truth which only love can understand and accept. To love someone does not mean to spoil him and make him a weakling, rather, love has in itself a true sense of education. It is demanding. Love sacrifices itself for others. It does not save them from sacrifice and temptation, from cross and illness, but rather, it enables and prepares an individual for life. In this way the love of a loved one and his response are tested, cleansed and mature. Remember, the mother who loves her child is the first to feel pain when she has to take her child to the hospital for an operation so that the child can be well again. She is not afraid of the suffering because she seeks the healing of her child. He who loves his garden will not leave it unattended, but trim it and weed it so that it can bear more fruit. So temptation and suffering have a purpose!

In the days when He was in the flesh, He offered prayers and supplications with loud cries and tears to the One who was able to save Him from death, and He was heard because of His reverence. Son

*though He was, He learned obedience through
what He suffered; and when He was made perfect,
He became the source of eternal salvation for all
who obey Him... (Heb. 5:7-9).*

* * * * * * *

LOVE YEARNS for the RECOGNITION
of a LOVED ONE

*Dear Children! You are a chosen people and
God has given you great graces. You do not comprehend every message which I am giving you.
Now I just want to say, pray, pray, pray! I don't
know what else to tell you because I love you and
I want you to comprehend my love and God's love
through prayer. Thank you for having responded
to my call* (November 15, 1984).

The one who loves is always in a personal meeting with
the one he loves. Love does not see the multitude of people
in an impersonal way. Love knows all people and decides
personally for everyone, and gives to each one personally.
This is the essence of love. If it does not give itself personally
to others, then it is not love. In giving itself, love and the
loved ones are fulfilling themselves; they grow, mature and
become able to love more and give more of themselves. Love,
therefore, cannot stop, because between the one who loves
and the one who is loved there is no one who loves last.
Love is eternal, and Heaven consists in giving and receiving
love. Therefore, to love means to yearn to know the loved
one more and more. He who loves God learns about Him
more and more, and loves Him all the more.

God's love, which manifests itself through Mary and
becomes her personal love, can be recognized through prayer,
because prayer is friendship with God. A response to Divine
Love and to Mary's motherly love is born and grows through
prayer. What is not known cannot be loved. So also, the
growth of a person as an individual consists in recognizing,

11

accepting, and responding to the Divine recognition in love. That is then the life which is stronger than death, because there is no death between loved ones. Where there is no love and recognition, there is already death, darkness and destruction.

Mary is showing us the way. We need to pray and personally to decide for prayer. When it is hard for us to pray, and when we find reasons not to pray, then we are always in danger of deceiving ourselves and others. He who has no time for prayer does not love God and he is not growing in God's presence. Hardship in prayer does not have to be a negative sign. On the contrary, it can be a new proof that we love and in spite of the difficulty and hardship, we are trying to grow in the presence of God.

> *I am the good shepherd. A good shepherd lays down his life for the sheep...I am the good shepherd; I know my sheep, and my sheep know me, just as the Father knows Me and I know the Father, and I will lay down My life for the sheep (Jn. 10:11,14-15).*

* * * * * * *

TO KNOW, or NOT KNOW HOW to LOVE

> *Dear Children! No, you don't know how to love and you do not know how to listen with love to the words I am saying to you. Be conscious, my beloved, that I am your Mother and I have come on earth to teach you to listen out of love, to pray out of love and not compelled by the fact that you are carrying a cross. By means of the cross God is glorified through every person. Thank you for having responded to my call* (November 29, 1984).

Many people are asking themselves why apparitions, and why in Medjugorje? Why every day? The questions are legitimate. Sometimes people disregard apparitions because of just such questions. To ask with love and to seek the response with love is all that can be hoped for, because the answers cannot be accepted by force!

To a mother who loves, only one concern is important. She wants what is good for us so that there will be no forcefulness among us and especially, between us and her. Love and force cannot go together. They are as opposite in themselves as are light and darkness, or truth and falsehood. Force closes the approach to love. It closes the mouth, the ears, the heart and the whole being. Love however, talks, responds, listens, offers itself freely and awaits a response in freedom. When a person frees himself from inner forces which are the result of a dependence on material goods or on a false perception of self and others and becomes truly free, then the outer forces become an opportunity to demonstrate the inner freedom and personal decision.

The world is full of slavery and, therefore, full of enslaved souls and hearts. We are enslaved by selfishness and conceit, enslaved because of our own desires and passions toward money, drugs, alcohol, immoral lifestyles and immoral relationships. Many are enslaved by the direct influence of satanic action which is expressed by sin. And, the slavery to the fear of suffering is especially widespread.

On one occasion I asked Jelena Vasilj how she discerns the voice of Our Lady from that of Satan. She answered, "When Our Lady speaks, I have time for answering. I am free. I have space in my soul and I can decide. When Satan speaks, I feel pressured, He does not leave time to think. He wants to interfere and deceive and I feel pushed to the corner..."

> For you were called for freedom, brothers. But
> do not use this freedom as an opportunity for the
> flesh; rather serve one another through love. For
> the whole law is fulfilled in one statement, namely,
> "You shall love your neighbor as yourself." But
> if you go on biting and devouring one another,
> beware that you are not consumed by one another
> (Gal. 5:13-15).

LOVE and JOY

Dear Children! You know that the season of joy is getting closer, but without love you will achieve nothing. So first of all, begin to love your own family and everyone in the parish, and then you will be able to love and accept all who come here. Now let these seven days be a week when you need to learn to love. Thank you for having responded to my call (December 13, 1984).

This message was given during Advent time. Christmas is the time of joy, and joy is the fruit of love. Every human heart yearns deeply for joy. Sadness, disappointment, failure, emptiness, inner-desert dryness are the realities which every human heart wants to avoid or to overcome as soon as possible. There is always the danger that a person will try to achieve joy without love, and this is, without exception, a distraction to self and to others. To decide for love means to decide for joy. Joy is born in the human heart and it dwells there, when the heart is open to others, responding to their love and "earning" with its love, their trust. Trust can bring on suffering but does not kill joy. Mistrust, however, always brings sadness and insecurity, for it breaks what is needed for life in the heart of a loved one.

Love gives us the promise that we will achieve everything with it. However, it really begins with self. To educate ourselves in the rules of life, as we experience them in a pure heart, the way God planted them and to remain faithful to these rules, is to have joy. To betray these inner rules, means we walk the way of sadness and anguish.

Love is a grace. It is a gift to man. Man by himself did not invent the necessity for love, because it was born within him. However, love is also a fruit of cooperation with grace, a fruit of our exercising freely our will in accepting this inner law by the growing and spreading of love. One needs to start immediately, today, and continue every day, every week, every year. And then we will be ready for Christmas. Every moment is a moment of grace. Every day is a gift, an assignment and a call to grow in love. Every day is filled with purpose if we respond to this call, and if not, the day remains empty. The exercises through which love grows are daily forgiveness and reconciliation, not judging, giving gifts, enjoying the gifts, fighting against negative feelings and opening our hearts for others. Whoever does so is in constant preparation for Christmas and he lives constantly in Christmas until, one day, he is transferred to an eternal Christmas, to happy eternity, where love reigns and through love eternal joy.

If I speak in human and angelic tongues but do not have love, I am a resounding gong, or a clashing cymbal. And if I have a gift of prophecy and comprehend all mysteries and all knowledge; if I had all faith. . . but do not have love, I gain nothing (1 Cor. 13:1-2).

*   *   *   *   *   *   *

LOVE SEES and SPEAKS

Dear Children! Today also I want to thank you for your sacrifices. And especially I want to thank those who are dear to my heart and like to come here. There are many parishioners who are not listening to the messages, but because of those who are in a special way close to my heart, because of them I am giving messages for the parish. And I will go on giving them because I love you and I want you to spread my messages with your heart. Thank you for having responded to my call (January 10, 1985).

Love is grateful. It does not forget and it is not blind to the sacrifices of those who love. Sacrifice and sacrificial offerings render joy and love, security and peace in the hearts of those for whom they are offered. Sacrifice produces gratefulness and joy in the heart of the one for whom it is offered, and it gives strength to endure to the person offering the sacrifice.

We are not in accordance with love when we are blind to the sacrifices of another, sacrifices offered out of love. This blindness often brings suffering. When children are not grateful to parents for their sacrifices and when they forget them or ignore them, they will be asking for more sacrifices. There is great suffering for both. Ungratefulness and ignorance of the love which is rooted in divine love, can present a new opportunity to demonstrate that love. Love is ongoing and inventive. When it comes to the blind and deaf who do not see and do not hear, love does not stop, but continues to love and remain in action.

Our Lady is grateful to those in the parish who listen and respond with sacrifices produced by love. Even when some do not listen, she continues to speak because she sees those souls who do listen. Her words pronounced with love caused a new relationship in the heart of a listener. They renew him and he becomes a witness. He who experiences divine love and the love of Mother Mary will receive a new word in his heart. The word will stay with him in his spiritual growth and he will be able to spread it at every moment by living the word which was said to him. So, love creates a word in the heart and opens up the eyes, while hate kills the word, closes the eyes and makes a person blind. In his blindness, one can destroy himself and bring evil to others.

Mary speaks as a Mother and she wants to create love in the hearts of her children. This love is not afraid of sacrifice, and the sacrifice demonstrates love. This is a condition for new life.

If we realize that the above message was given at the beginning of a new year, in January, we can better comprehend the program which Mary is implementing and wants to realize in our hearts.

Love is patient, love is kind. It is not jealous, it is not pompous, it is not inflated, it is not rude, it does not seek its own interests, it is not quick-tempered, it does not brood over injury, it does not rejoice over wrongdoing but rejoices with the truth. It bears all things, believes all things, hopes all things, endures all things (1 Cor. 13:4-7).

*   *   *   *   *   *   *

THE MOVING POWER of LOVE

Dear Children! From day to day I have been inviting you to a renewal of prayer in the parish, but you are not accepting it. Today I am calling you for the last time! Now it is Lent and you as a parish can turn to my message during Lent out of love. If you don't do that, I do not wish to keep on giving messages. God is approving this. Thank you, for having responded to my call (February 21, 1985).

The person who loves is active, busy, encouraged and tireless. For love in itself is a power in the one who loves, moving him towards the one whom he loves. The activity of love is the communication between loved ones. Love is alive, courageous. It embraces the situation as it is and tries to move the loved one to growth and betterment and to pull him out of laziness, which is a resistance to love. Therefore, the one who loves often suffers and is sad when he finds resistance or a lack of response. Then love has to become courageous. It may withdraw, walk away, and discontinue dialogue, not in order to punish, but rather, to try to open the eyes and the heart of the loved one. Love is inventive and uses all the means of space and time, customs and situations, to move the loved person.

Lent is the time of renewal. It is a time of conversion and return, a time of awakening from a mortal dream to a new life, a new life through love. The time of Lent begins in the winter and ends in the spring. It begins with a sorrowful passion and ends with a glorious resurrection. If the loved one does not awaken, then love can become silent in order to create a new condition for communication. Love is tireless. Here we think of a mother's love. How many times does a mother threaten her child in order to help him realize her love. Our Lady is busy and tireless, courageous and inventive, because she loves. She has moved many, through the events in Medjugorje, to follow the way in which her love is leading them. She is happy for them and patiently waits for those who do not listen. She invites all who have heard, to pray and become witnesses, so that all can gather in the Father's house of life and peace.

> *Realize how far you have fallen. Repent and do the works you did at first. Otherwise, I will come to you and remove your lampstand from its place, unless you repent* (*Rev.* 2:5).

*   *   *   *   *   *   *

POSSIBLE and IMPOSSIBLE

> *Dear Children! Today I call you to live this week by the words, "I love God!" Dear children, through love you will achieve everything and even what you think is impossible. God wants this parish to belong completely to him. And that is what I want too. Thank you for having responded to my call* (February 28, 1985).

Love is a grace and a gift from God which can spread only if an individual accepts and cooperates with the grace. Love is a seed entrusted to a human, planted in his heart. The seed can grow only if there is cooperation, only if there is a daily feeding which can be used in every situation. To find good guidance and to implement the correct practice means to mature and become strong. The purpose is clear, love towards God. The way is simple and concrete. Take one day and practice living the words, "I love God!" There is no need to talk much about this exercise. The more we talk about the exercise and do not practice it, the more we will not have results. Perhaps this is often the fate of God's love and its seed which has been entrusted to us. We talk much about love, but practice it little. We know the rules well, but we do not implement them! Let us now try to do so.

The first exercise is Prayer. "Oh God, thank You for the love by which You love me!" After each invocation, remain a few moments in silence, repeating it in your heart. Repeat it every day until your heart begins to direct the prayers by itself. That means, if the mind forgets, then the heart forms the words by itself! Yes, the practice of prayer then becomes a deep part of our being and a necessity of the heart. If we forget to pray, we immediately begin to suffocate just as we would suffocate if we forgot to breathe.

"God, today I wish to love you with all my life, with my successes and my failures, in meeting with people and nature.

God, I love you in the members of my family, my community... (mention names).

God I love you in those with whom I fight, hate... (mention names).

God, I wish to love you constantly. Increase my love.

God, when I forget You, awaken in me an ardent desire to love You.

God, when my strength is at its end, grant that my heart may cry out and respond with love.

God, when my love falls short, help me to love You with the love of Mary, Your humble servant.

Mary, Mother of Love, pray for me every day, every week throughout my whole life."

Then the King will say to those on His right, "Come, you blessed by my Father. Inherit the kingdom prepared for you from the foundation of the world. For I was hungry and you gave me food, I was thirsty and you gave me drink, a stranger and you welcomed me, named and you clothed Me, ill and you cared for Me, in prison and you visited Me" ...Amen, I say to you, whatever you did for one of these least brothers of Mine, you did it for Me (Mt. 25:34-36,40).

*   *   *   *   *   *   *

THAT IT BE GOOD

Dear Children! I wish to keep on giving messages and therefore today I call you to live and accept my messages! Dear children, I love you and in a special way I have chosen this parish, one more dear to me than the others, in which I have gladly remained when the Almighty sent me. Therefore I invite you to accept me, dear children, that it might go well with you. Listen to my messages! Thank you for having responded to my call (March 21, 1985).

Mary speaks. She speaks because she loves. She, as a mother, loves her own and all who are hers. She gives messages which the love in her heart produces and inspires. Speech has its own task. Because words, when spoken with love, create a response, even if they do not find a response in the very beginning. Mary is a mother who gives birth spiritually to children. She implants her speech, her words and her love in order to give birth to a response in the hearts of her own. A man often stops talking if he does not receive a response, because man's speech is conditional. God speaks and, by talking, He creates. Such is the word of Mary, because God, Himself, entrusted her to talk. She speaks, and by her speech, she causes movement. She patiently awaits the birth of a response in the hearts of her own.

God's word, sent to earth, would not return until it brought fruit. The word has its rules, its way. It has as its purpose to incarnate into a human, to create a new word. Therefore, the word is spoken. It is announced by those who open up to Mary and by those in whom it is incarnated. Mary, in a special way, gave space to the Word. Therefore, she can speak. All those who are renewed by the Word, begin to experience it and become like the one from whom they received the Word. To hear, to accept the Word, to give a response, to become the Word would be good for all of us. Today, many are deaf to the Word and therefore, mute because they have nothing to say. That is why there is so much misunderstanding in our world, and why so many are misunderstood and tossed aside. And this is not good.

Mary is God's word to us. In her the Word became flesh; it became reality. She is the most beautiful word of God to this world. It is the mother's word now which moves to many. In her, God is explaining Himself to the world. She is our teacher. She is a new creature, a new star, who speaks about God's plans. She is an invitation into new times and it would be good for us to accept her, the virgin, incarnate with the Faithful One. Our way is like hers, to be God's word to others. She will be the new Heaven and the new earth.

> *Whoever loves me will keep my word, and my Father will love him and we will come to him and make our dwelling with him. Whoever does not love me does not keep my words; yet the word you hear is not mine, but that of the Father who sent me. I have told you this while I am with you. The Advocate, the Holy Spirit, that the Father will send in my name, He will teach you everything and remind you of all that I have told you (Jn. 14:23-26).*

* * * * * * *

ACCEPT and LOVE

> *Dear Children! During these days people from all nations will be coming into the parish. And now I am calling you to love. Love first of all those in your household and then you will be able to accept and love all who are coming. Thank you for having responded to my call (June 6, 1985).*

The parish of St. James is chosen. The visionaries are chosen. People are chosen. Choosing is a proof of love. And love, given as a gift, deserves a response because love is the most beautiful Word of God and word about God. When

God's Love, as His Word, creates a new word in a human being, then it causes love toward self, toward our own, towards all people and toward all creatures. This new word, pronounced by words and deeds, becomes a witness. Many will come to this parish. All who come are called and chosen. They come to the Mother who speaks and who testifies through those who first experienced being chosen (the visionaries), who heard the word and became a new word for all the chosen ones. Those who come have heard the word and have responded. They wish to accept and to answer. Parishioners are called, then, to testify with love. This testimony begins in the home with their own, with their dear ones and those they live with and come in contact with daily. Often there are not enough words of love from them and the power of testimony diminishes. From there the power of words will begin to transmit and encompass all who must go forth as lighted lamps, spreading a new voice of God to the world from which they come. So, the success of God's talk and Mary's word depends upon the response of parishioners and the whole parish. What a joy that God talks to us in this way through Mary! And what a responsibility we have before God and before Mary for others!

To accept Our Lady's messages, to accept others and love them the way Mary accepts and loves them, means to partake in the role of a mother in giving birth to a new word. There is no other way, nor could there be another way. The experience of pilgrims and parishioners is indeed a new experience of togetherness. All who come to this parish community, come to experience it as their own. They experience being members of a greater community, the Church, to which Mary is Mother and each person is a loved child.

There is, however, a constant danger, that Mary's words become ordinary, everyday talk, which do not move and do not create new witnesses. There is also the danger of the witnesses becoming tired, because they are hearing so many words from the world and so many tempting melodies that they become deaf to the Divine Word. By praying and fasting and by constant cleansing, this danger can be overcome. When we discover brothers and sisters in our neighbors, the dear children of the same Mother, and we love and accept them we witness in a joyful way. We all become joyfully responsible for God's love and the increase of love in the world.

> *Put on then, as God's chosen ones, holy and beloved, heartfelt compassion, kindness, humility, gentleness and patience...And over all these, put on love, that is, the bond of perfection* (Col. 3:12,14).

* * * * * * *

WITH PEACE, JOY, and LOVE

> *Dear Children! For this holy day I wish to tell you to open your hearts to the Lord of all hearts. Give me all your feelings and all your problems. I wish to comfort you in all your trials. I wish to fill you with peace, joy, and the love of God. Thank you for having responded to my call* (June 20, 1985).

Human happiness is unthinkable without peace in the heart. Peace gives birth to a deep security and the heart is joyful. A joyful heart is open to love, and love increases joy and peace. Peace, love, and joy are certainly the deepest desires of every human heart. Therefore, a human being tries to do everything to achieve that **peace** which gives birth to joy, and which in turn, increases love.

Mary is pointing out to us the divine way to this peace, joy, and love. The first condition is an openness to God, for He is the spring of peace and joy and love. He is the creator and also the Lord of hearts. To open oneself does not mean anything more than to accept His love, to allow His love to flow into the heart with peace and, in a daily encounter with God, allow His peace, joy, and love to grow. Mary knows that our emotions and problems can become obstacles to openness to God. Therefore, she is inviting us to give her our feelings, everything that bothers us, even things that

23

make us happy. Because success and failure, health and illness, riches and poverty, all can become obstacles to our opening up to God. They can become fateful obstacles on the way toward peace.

Mary, as a mother, not only wants to give birth to life, but she wants to teach us how to live. Therefore, she calls us to entrust everything to her, as to a mother. To know how to entrust your feelings and problems to someone is a great wisdom of life. If you do not open up to God and people in that way, you fall into loneliness. You remain separated from others, become an inmate of the dungeon which you have created and in which you punish yourself. This then, is a human tragedy as with a seed which rots away when it does not open up itself to the sun and rain.

Each one of us needs consolation, human and divine. If we only want peace, joy, and love on a human level and by human ways, then we accept the way of betrayal and disappointment. A person enchanted by this world excludes a divine awareness in himself and prepares a stage in which he has to be disappointed. It becomes again a moment for seeking divine consolation, divine peace and love. Happy are all those who hear the offer that God, through Mary, wants to fill them with peace, joy, and love, so that they can open themselves to this offer and accept its conditions.

> *In contrast, the fruit of the Spirit is love, joy, peace, patience, kindness, generosity, faithfulness, gentleness, self-control. Against such there is no law. Now those who belong to Christ Jesus have crucified their flesh with its passions and desires. If we live in the Spirit, we also follow the Spirit (Gal. 5:22-25).*

*　*　*　*　*　*　*

HUMBLY with LOVE

Dear Children! Today I am giving you a message through which I desire to call you to humility. These days you have felt great joy because of all the people who have come and to whom you could tell your experiences with love. Now I invite you to continue in humility and with an open heart speak to all who are coming. Thank you for having responded to my message (June 28, 1985).

This message was given in 1985 as a gift after the solemn celebration of the fourth anniversary of the apparitions. The anniversary was somehow a great and powerful breakthrough of the message of peace into the world and the beginning of an enormous response from the whole world. It was a joyful happening for the parish community, because parishioners became aware that they were not alone. There was a feeling of victory and this caused celebration. The existing communist system opened itself and reached out, as was said, after "Our Lady's cake!" This was on a material level. Still, it was important that everyone was able to breathe more easily.

Something positive happened among the church people, the church hierarchy. Many publicly demonstrated that they were interested in the happenings in the parish. Joy was growing because we witnessed that God's action was growing through Mary. Parishioners felt the victory and joyfully talked about everything they experienced during the last four years.

Mary, as a teacher and mother, knows that every success can be blinding. And when blindness leads to pride then it's easy to forget that we are only tools in God's hands, that all we have is only the sign of God's confidence in us. When we forget this, then we are in the center and God loses His place. That is pride! Pride pushes God out of our words, our thoughts and our actions. Wherever there is no room for God, God steps back. Then there is no room for man either and so he loses his life's space.

Mary, a humble servant of the Lord, knows what all this means and, therefore she calls for humility. Humility creates a deep sense of self as gift, of others as gift and of God as gift-giver. Humility is the joyful acceptance of cooperation with God and the conscious decision to be a tool in His hands. This does not deny the individual, but rather it puts things in their proper place. Therefore, the visionaries, the parish staff, the whole parish, and the numerous witnesses spread throughout the whole world are called to a humble awareness of God from whom all good comes and a true understanding of self and self merits. This is the way of joy and peace!

For by the grace given to me, I tell everyone among you not to think of himself more highly than one ought to think, but to think soberly, each according to the measure of faith that God has apportioned...Let love be sincere; hate what is evil, hold on to what is good; love one another with mutual affection, anticipate one another in showing honor. Do not grow slack in zeal, be fervent in spirit, serve the Lord (Rom. 12:3,9-11).

*　*　*　*　*　*　*

SACRIFICE OFFERED with LOVE

Dear Children! I thank you for every sacrifice you have offered. And now I urge you to offer every sacrifice with love. I wish you to help those who are helpless, to begin helping with confidence and the Lord will keep on giving you confidence. Thank you for having responded to my call (July 4, 1985).

In her messages, Our Lady has asked for and continues to ask for sacrifice. However, it is not simple to define what sacrifice is. According to our perception, sacrifice is not measured by the same measures which we are accustomed to use. Rather, it is measured by love. The greater the love, the less difficult the sacrifice will seem. And if there is no love, then everything becomes hard and everything is a sacrifice. We can call "sacrifice" a situation or action in which one person applies himself, his time, or his life for others. The more a person is free from his own self, the more he will be able to sacrifice himself for others. We begin to sacrifice ourselves when we love someone. Without love sacrifice is impossible and unthinkable. And with love, sacrifice loses its unpleasantness.

Christ has been sacrificing for us from the beginning. He gives His life and His cross as a gift to the Father for us. His action is redemptive because He did it all without pressure, but with love, freely. Mary, in her school, asks for prayer, fasting, confession, Holy Mass, reading of the Sacred Scriptures. She wants us to help others, to give our life for them. She asks for sacrifice, but with love. She thanks us for all our actions that are done with love.

Love makes every action, even the smallest ones, enormously valuable. With the help of love, even our smallest deeds become great acts in the eyes of God. We often face the danger of forgetting the importance of our own actions and sacrifices, and we feel helpless and unworthy. But we can overcome this helplessness with love, and then our sacrifices take on enormous value. He who loves, is not helpless. He is close to God and close to others. This produces confidence.

This richness we carry in clay containers, so that an exceptional success is attributed to God, and not to us. In everything we suffer hardships, but we are not in anguish; we do not know where to turn, but we do not despair; we are persecuted, but we are not abandoned in danger; they are knocking us down on earth, but we are not destroyed. We, always and everywhere on our body, carry the mortal suffering of Jesus, that the life of Jesus can be manifested on our body. We are always giving ourselves to death for as long as we live, because of Jesus, that the life of Jesus can be revealed on our mortified body.

And so: death manifests its power in us, and life its power in you (2 Cor. 4:7-12).

*   *   *   *   *   *   *

I LOVE YOU

Dear Children! Today I am blessing you and I wish to tell you that I love you and that I urge you to live my messages. Today I am blessing you with the solemn blessing that the Almighty has given me. Thank you for having responded to my call (August 15, 1985).

Every mother is an educator. She not only gives physical birth, but she continues to give spiritual birth, and she follows the spiritual growth of her child. Therefore, she repeats her thoughts with her words and gives emphasis to them. Only love can understand this repetition. It is interesting to note that one who loves tirelessly keeps repeating and confirming love and devotion to the loved person. Also, the loved person wants to hear repetitious proofs of love. Never has anyone complained about expressions of love with the words, "I heard that already," or "You said this," or "You did that already." More often the opposite happens. We complain when the proofs of love are missing.

Mary, as mother, knows what her children need. She lives by the power of love. She educates. This is why she repeats her messages. The above message was given to us on the great feast of the Assumption. That feast day is solemn for all her children and not only for the children, but for the Mother as well. The visionaries confirm that on her feast days she comes in a festive gown and is joyful. On this feast day, a multitude of people had gathered from all over the world. She is happy and she gives a blessing, showing her motherly love over and over again. This is an opportunity to tell her children to live in harmony with her messages.

God Himself is observing this and is glorified through Mary's Assumption. He clothed her in the sun, with the moon under her feet, and He surrounded her with stars. He allows special blessings. Joy is obvious. Her joy produces love and is born of love. And this is the way of peace.

Sing to the Lord a new song of praise in the assembly of the faithful.
Let Israel be glad in its Creator,
Let the children of Zion rejoice in their King.
Let them praise His name in the festive dance,
Let them sing praise to Him with a drum and harp.
For Yahweh loves His people and He adorns the lowly with victory.
Let the faithful exult in glory;
Let them sing for joy upon their couches
(Ps. 149:1-5).

*   *   *   *   *   *   *

PEACEFULLY and with LOVE THROUGH TEMPTATIONS

Dear Children! Today I wish to tell you that God wants to send you trials which you can overcome by prayer. God is testing you through daily chores. Now pray to withstand peacefully every trial. From everything through which God tests you come out more open to God and approach Him with love. Thank you for having responded to my call (August 22, 1985).

"And lead us not into temptation, but deliver us from the evil one." This is our daily prayer. We ask over and over again, "Does God tempt us? Does He send temptations to His people?" In order to answer this question, we would need to discuss and explain it in great detail. However, one thing is certain. Jesus put the words of His prayer into our mouths.

Mary, in her message, says that God is testing, that He is sending temptations. While we leave this question for further discussion, let us not forget that in the message, something very important which we do not accept so easily is stated. Temptations are opportunities in which we can show our faithfulness. We can conquer temptations with prayer and everything can be turned to good. This then, is what, in this moment, interests Our Lady as mother and educator. She does not explain why it is so, but she shows us the way and the good which can come out of it.

Everything that happens to us is known to God. Nothing can happen to us without His will. When we suffer we wonder if it could be God's will that we suffer this or that, or that our family suffers, or our nation suffers. Suffering is a school and God can lead us through this school. This is why Mary is here. Trials and temptations are an invitation either to return to God or to open ourselves more to Him so that we do not set ourselves into our own programs, lest we get lost in our ways. Through temptations, human intentions are being cleansed. Therefore, instead of the word "temptation," we could use "means of education."

It is possible through temptation to walk peacefully with love! God is with us even when testing comes as a direct result of our conduct, or sin. So then, the openness toward God grows. Days of temptation are the days of a special presence of God. This kind of experience produces peace. However, in order to comprehend this, one needs to pray and to experience peace.

> *Consider it all joy, my brothers, when you encounter various trials, for you know that the testing of your faith produces perseverance. And let perseverance be perfect, so that you may be perfect and complete, lacking in nothing (Jas. 1:2-4).*

*   *   *   *   *   *   *

TO CLEANSE the HEART with LOVE

Dear Children! Everything has its own time. Today I call you to start working on your own hearts. Now that all the work in the field is over, you are finding time for cleaning even the most neglected areas, but you leave your heart aside. Work more and clean with love every part of your heart. Thank you for having responded to my call (October 17, 1985).

A person has to grow, to develop and to mature. If this does not happen, then the person is dead. Just as a person's body has to grow and develop, so also the law for mental and spiritual advancement is valid. Sadly, however, mental and spiritual growth often do not follow the physical. In today's world and today's order of values, it happens frequently that a person neglects his mental and spiritual development and cares only about the physical and material. Therefore, we meet more and more people who are mentally and spiritually dead, stunted, or immature. The more material goods people have the more they are in danger of forgetting their spiritual development. It is true happiness when people accept their material blessedness as the foundation of spiritual and intellectual development. If this does not happen, then all sorts of human hardships begin. People feel inadequate for spiritual values.

Mary, as mother and teacher, reminds us not to lose our balance. That is the reason for her saying that we should work spiritually on our hearts, just as we work in the fields. In the fields, one must work thoroughly if he wishes to have fruit. Uncultivated land is a grove for every seed, even for the best ones. It is the same with a heart. We must fight thoroughly to pull out every evil root of selfishness, conceit, and laziness as well as the evil roots of every bad habit. We should cleanse our heart from these roots which are tying us to this world and making us become slaves. It is a task that must be thorough, continuous and daily. The person who does not work like this is not open to the Spirit, nor

31

can the gifts of the Spirit be rooted and grow in him. This work should be done with love. Without love, spiritual seedlings cannot succeed.

Therefore, this education is similar to working in the fields. It involves cleaning, weeding, trimming, tying the branch to a stronger plant, watering, and finally selecting the best fruit. It is not always easy. What is needed is knowledge, time, love, experience, reason, and the help of other people.

> *Make no mistake: God is not mocked, for a person will reap only what he sows. The one who sows for his flesh, will reap corruption from the flesh, but the one who sows for the Spirit will reap eternal life from the Spirit. Let us not grow tired of doing good, for in due time we shall reap our harvest, if we do not give up. So then, while we have the opportunity, let us do good to all, but especially to those who belong to the family of faith (Gal. 6:7-10).*

*   *   *   *   *   *   *

THE WAY to BEAUTY

> *Dear Children! From day to day I wish to clothe you in holiness, goodness, obedience, and God's love, so that from day to day you become more beautiful and more prepared for your Master. Dear children, listen to and live my messages. I wish to guide you. Thank you for having responded to my call (October 24, 1985).*

Every mother wants to dress her child well. Every mother wants to do everything to make her child more beautiful and be surrounded with beauty and good. The fact is that many parents in these days care only for the external beauty of their children. They would do anything for their child to have everything. This is good and this kind of care should not be neglected. In fact, negligence would mean irresponsibility.

However, if parental love only expresses itself on the material and external level then that love is inadequate, unjust and perilous for the child. The complete beauty of a person cannot be realized without spiritual beauty. For as much as we care for the material and external, so much and no less (if not more) should we care for the spiritual and inner beauty, for the development of the whole person.

Mary knows the parts of the spiritual dress of her children very well. That is the reason that she says she wants, from day to day, to clothe us in holiness, goodness, obedience, and in the love of God. Holiness is an expression of the spiritual state of a person, a manifestation of his spiritual and physical health and of his deep connection with God and with people. It is a state of total balance of spirit, soul, and body, when the law of spirit rules over the law of matter. A holy person is no longer alone or an outcast, but rather he experiences a new unity with God and with people. He is beautifully made ready for new encounters.

Goodness is a part of this spiritual dress through which one discovers the good in every creature. Through goodness a person can accept himself the way he is and others the way they are. He does not look down upon anyone. Goodness is the spiritual power through which a person overcomes evil temptations within himself. A good person will not judge nor will he condemn anyone. He will be ready to share his spiritual and material goods with everyone.

Obedience is that part of our spiritual dress which connects us with God the Creator and with His will. When we listen to the Word of God in humility and openness and try to recognize the will of God, then we are obedient. This is just the opposite of haughtiness which leads a person into not cooperating with God. Humbleness means accepting God's plan.

Love of God is that part of the spiritual dress which makes everything valuable and without which all would be empty. Mary was adorned with this kind of dress, and for this reason she is the most beautiful of all creatures. She wants all of her children to radiate this same beauty.

...put away the old self of your former way of life, corrupted through deceitful desires, and be renewed in the spirit of your minds, and put on the new self, created in God's way, in righteousness and holiness of truth (Eph. 4:22-24).

*　*　*　*　*　*　*

LOVE MAKES EVERYTHING VALUABLE

Dear Children! Today I wish to call you to work in the Church. I love all the same and I desire from each one to work as much as is possible. I know, dear children, that you can, but you do not wish to because you feel small and humble in these things. You need to be courageous and like little flowers and do your share for the Church and for Jesus so that everyone can be satisfied. Thank you for having responded to my call (October 31, 1985).

No one has an excuse. We are all loved with the same immeasurable measure. Love is the source of life's strength and action. Those who know they are loved, also know they are free, courageous and active. They are not afraid of their weaknesses or of other peoples' mistakes. Haughtiness is not driving them to false inaction. Love does not seek excuses, but rather acts. One who loves and who is loved is conscious of the fact that everything has enormous value because love makes every action great, both in human and in God's eyes. Also, they know that it is better to make mistakes by working than to avoid mistakes by being lazy.

Those who do not experience the love which surpasses their goodness or evilness, who are only rewarded for the good and punished for their mistakes, without love, are always insecure, stressed and anxious. They have to succeed at any price. They are without joy and peace. The only rules by which they measure themselves and others are their visible successes and human praise. But when praise is not given, it creates despair in their hearts or a lack of courage for further work. A great evil in today's lifestyle is being developed this way, and many people hurt indeed.

Mary is a Mother. She loves each child equally. Therefore each child is invited to respond and consciously contribute what he can, where he can. Church life is the life of unity. In this life everyone has his place, his irreplaceable place. No one can love in place of someone else. The little ones and the great, the healthy ones and the sick, the rich ones and the poor, the learned and the uneducated, all can and therefore must contribute to the life of a community.

Each flower in a bouquet is important. No one flower is more important or less important, but each one is indispensably valuable. What a joy for each member of the Church when he realizes and accepts this truth. How much bitterness would disappear from hearts, how much evil talk would cease, how many would be healed from a belief that they are inferior beings.

> *There are many kinds of spiritual gifts but the same Spirit; there are different forms of service but the same Lord; there are different accomplishments but the same God Who produces everything in everyone. To each individual the revelation of the Spirit is given for the benefit of all...As a body is one though it has many parts, and all the parts of the body, though many, are one body, so also is Christ (1 Cor. 12:4-7,12).*

* * * * * * *

BARRIERS are SURMOUNTED THROUGH LOVE

Dear Children! I am calling you to the love of neighbor and love toward the one from whom evil comes to you. In that way with love you will be able to discern the intentions of hearts. Pray and love, Dear Children! By love you are able to do even that which you think is impossible. Thank you for having responded to my call (November 7, 1985).

Our human experience confirms that every human being wants to be loved. Animals and plants also respond positively to love. To be loved and to love is a fundamental law of life and living. Where there is no love, there is hate, and where there is hate there is death and destruction. To love and to be loved means to have a light in your heart, and with that light to see and recognize people and events. However, when one begins to hate and does not respond with love but rather distances himself or becomes judgmental, death creeps in.

Death first takes hold of those who hate, even if on a human level they find reason and justification for their hatred. First, those who hate suffer. The human response is always to love those who love and to hate those who hate, to return with the same measure, a tooth for a tooth, a wound for a wound, a bomb for a bomb. This is a law of death, which is, unfortunately, closer to us than the law of life.

Mary wants to lead us on a different way, the way of Christ, the way of the children of God and the way of her children. She wants to teach us to win over hatred with love, to conquer darkness with light and to overcome insult with forgiveness. This is where Christ's love begins and Christian love as well. The one who loves is in the light. Love becomes a means by which human intentions are revealed. Love discerns but does not condemn. Love understands and accepts and does not cast away. Love, therefore, often seems naive and helpless, while it is indeed all-powerful. The one who loves becomes a partaker of divine power and divine knowledge. The one who does not love, loses all these abilities, because hatred is truly darkness. The one who does not love, punishes himself first of all and hinders his human development. He narrows his opportunities and shrinks his living space. Mary is trying to teach us the rules of life. That is the reason she invites us to love and through love to overcome human rationality and human logic.

Love is patient, love is kind. Love is not jealous, it is not conceited, it is not inflated. It is not rude, it does not seek its own interest, it is not quick-tempered, it does not brood over injury. It does not rejoice over wrongdoing but rejoices with truth. It bears all things, believes all things, hopes all things, endures all things. Love never ends (1 Cor. 13:4-8a).

* * * * * * *

LOVE OVERCOMES FATIGUE and DISTANCE

Dear Children! I, your Mother, love you and wish to urge you to prayer. I am tireless, dear children, and I am calling you even when you are far away from my heart. I am a Mother, and even though I feel pain for each one who goes astray, I forgive easily and am happy for every child who returns to me (November 14, 1985).

The one who loves is tireless in the search for the loved one. When we love by Christ's standard and by His power, human obstacles such as hatred, envy, jealousy, offenses, injustice, rejection, and unacceptance do not destroy us, but confirm our love. The one who loves discovers opportunities in which his love confirms and strengthens itself. Human love easily stops, grows tired, disappoints, and develops into a bad desire for revenge. When there is no response to human love, there is an emptiness from which the strongest forms of hatred are born. This love is nourished by human food only and seeks acknowledgement and compensation and sets up conditions. Often this kind of love grows tired and develops into hate. This is, surely, the moment when we question ourselves regarding our relations towards others. If other people often disappoint us and cause us to be disturbed or angry, then it does not mean that others are bad, but perhaps we expect too much from them because our love is only human.

37

Mary, as the Mother of beautiful love, wants to educate us for Christ's unconditional, powerful, tireless love. She is an example. In this message, for instance, she admits pain but not anger. She suffers on account of us because she loves us, but nevertheless, she intercedes for us. She is tireless, because her love is not conditioned by our response. She loves us even when we are far away. And she rejoices whenever we come back, when we convert. No one and nothing can close the door to her love and no one can be far from her, because she wants to be close to all. Love throws aside all barriers and removes all obstacles. In this way, Mary shows herself as the one in whom the Divine Love has found a proper place.

If we have grown tired within ourselves, in our family, community, society, in prayer, in doing good deeds, then that speaks, first of all, about the kind of love we have. The fatigue which manifests itself today in the world in different ways, such as in drugs, alcoholism, murder, suicide, and divorce is the best proof that true love needs to gain the green light again in the life of each individual. Then the evil in the individual, in families, in the Church and in the world can be overcome. This is the message of peace which comes through true love.

> *Set me as a seal on your heart, as a seal on your arm. For stern as death is love, relentless as the nether world is devotion; its flames are a blazing fire of Yahweh. Deep waters cannot quench love, nor floods sweep it away. Were one to offer all he owns to purchase love, he would be roundly mocked* (*Song* 8:6-7).

*   *   *   *   *   *   *

TO BECOME ALIKE THROUGH LOVE

Dear Children! I want to tell you that this season is especially for you from the parish. When it is summer, you say that you have a lot of work. Now you don't have work in the fields, work on your own self personally! Come to Mass because this is the season given to you. Dear children, there are enough of those who come regularly despite bad weather because they love me and wish to show their love in a special way. What I want from you is to show me your love by coming to Mass, and the Lord will reward you abundantly (November 21, 1985).

When we love someone, we do everything to be with the person and to spend time with the one we love. Love is the path to the other person and love inspires us to become like the loved one, and the loved one becomes like the one who loves. In this way we become subconsciously similar to the one we love. Love makes time shorter and every work and effort becomes easier when the meeting with the loved one is realized.

God loves man and He could not manifest His love in any other way but to create man in His image. God wants man to be like him in everything. God's love is demanding of man just because God loves. Jesus wants us to be merciful as the Heavenly Father is merciful. He wants us to be like Him, holy and blameless, and to love as He loves. To enable man to achieve this, God transforms Himself into nourishing bread, through Jesus Christ, to become life for man, to become like Him. Christ did this by coming among men, by becoming like men in everything but sin.

Mary wants to guide us toward love and to accompany us in our development. Therefore, in this message she invites us to come to Mass out of love for her. Her mission is to help us so that from day to day we may become like God through love. Our development in love is her glory, which she in turn hands over to God's honor. Her guidance would not be complete if she did not teach us to celebrate the Mass, for the Mass is indeed the most beautiful part of her school.

The one who loves will have time, and whoever does not love will always find an excuse not to come. When one does not come, he not only does not receive but he loses what he already has. Holy Mass enriches a person with a divine richness. The daily intention of our prayers could be simply that the Lord opens our eyes to the richness of the Eucharistic sacrifice so that through it we can grow as He wishes us to grow.

> *But rather, love your enemies and do good to them, and lend, expecting nothing back; then your reward will be great and you will be children of the Most High, for He Himself is kind to the ungrateful and the wicked. Be merciful, just as your Father is merciful. Stop judging, and you will not be judged. Stop condemning and you will not be condemned. Forgive and you will be forgiven* (*Lk.* 6:35-37).

*　*　*　*　*　*　*

IN PENANCE, PRAYER, and ACTS of LOVE

> *Dear Children! I am calling you to prepare yourselves for Christmas by means of penance, prayer and works of charity. Dear children, do not look toward material things, because then you will not be able to experience Cl ristmas. Thank you for having responded to my call* (December 5, 1985).

The fullness of the Christian life consists in love that produces good deeds. Penance, unfortunately, is often regarded as negative in Christian life and so people avoid penance. But penance concerns nothing more than the battle of the inner person against sin which tries to enslave us and make us unfit for action. Penance is a constant freeing of self from the negative influences in one's life and in the world.

This battle for freedom has its rules and regulations as does every battle. How much we will be ready to fight against haughtiness, selfishness, greed, lust, stinginess, laziness, offensiveness, unforgiveness, and jealousy depends upon our love of the freedom of the children of God. Practice in humbleness, obedience, simpleness, and forgiveness can be called a penance. Therefore penance is not something sad, but rather something joyful and very necessary for each person. Penance is similar to the keeper of a vineyard who comes in the spring and trims all the branches from the vines in order to enable the development of a good vineyard. If someone did not know what was going on, he would wonder what the keeper of the vineyard was doing.

The best way to know what we should trim from our heart is through prayer. Prayer is a meeting with God. God is light and in His light we can see our light as well, but in prayer we can also see our darkness. Through prayer we receive the strength to fight against self gain and the energy through which we can free ourselves.

Mary is calling us to penance, to prayer, and to acts of love. Christmas is a joyous event which can and should happen every day. Each time evil and sin die within us, when we pull them out of our heart, God can be born and dwell within us, and it is Christmas again. Without inner freedom there can be no Christmas for any individual. Freedom is freeing us for encounters with others, to see them, to help them by our actions of love, and by doing this we help ourselves the most. If we remain on the material level, we cannot experience Christmas.

What good is it, my brothers, if someone says he has faith but does not have works? Can that faith save him? If a brother or sister has nothing to wear and has no food for the day and one of you says to them, "Go in peace, keep warm, and eat well," but you do not give them the necessities of the body, what good is it? So also, faith of itself, if it does not have works, is dead...Demonstrate your faith to me apart from works, and I will demonstrate my faith to you through my works (*Jas.* 2:14-17,18b).

*   *   *   *   *   *   *

MEETING with JESUS BY LOVING YOUR NEIGHBOR

Dear Children! Today I wish to call you to love towards your neighbor and you will feel Jesus more, especially at Christmas. God will reward you with great gifts if you abandon yourselves to Him. I wish to give my motherly blessing in a special way to mothers on Christmas, and others will be blessed by Jesus with His blessing. Thank you for having responded to my call (December 19, 1985).

This is a Christmas message. From our Christian teaching we know that we meet God in our neighbor. Every person whom we meet or with whom we live, especially the sick, the helpless and the needy, offers us an opportunity to meet God. Life becomes a sacrament. However, we might pass by and not experience the deep meeting with God. Our neighbor can become for us either our temple, our paradise, or our Hell. The greatness and beauty of this Christian teaching consists precisely in this, but it is also a constant danger. God is close to people through Jesus Christ. His name is *Emmanuel,* God with us. Christians are not pantheists who believe everything is God, but Christians meet God in everyone, and by loving God, they love the people around them. By loving people they are on the path closest to God.

Mary prepares us for Christmas. Just as she gave the gift of the Incarnate Word to the world, she wants each of us to be blessed with an abundance of gifts. But, indeed, the best gift is God Himself, Who becomes both the gift and the giver.

In the message Mary promises her blessing to mothers. To bless means to speak well about someone, to accept someone, to create an atmosphere in which God can be met. A mother's blessing should be the one which enables mothers to accept, guard and love life, so that in children they meet and accept God. Jesus gives His blessing to everyone. He is the greatest blessing, Who did not come to judge, but to save. He did not come to hurt anyone, but to heal. When a human heart opens with joy to such a God, then He can enrich it. This is the great joy of Christmas. Hearts open up to the Good News even in the saddest moments, and joy opens hearts toward God and toward man.

Mary wants to accomplish a joyful unity among her children who still suffer greatly because they are far from Christmas, far from one another. The peace which she calls us to means closeness and warmth.

> *This saying is trustworthy. I want you to insist on these points, that those who have believed in God be careful to devote themselves to good works; this is good and beneficial to people (Ti. 3:8).*

* * * * * * *

A WORD AT the END of the YEAR

> *Dear Children! I wish to thank all who have listened to my messages and who on Christmas Day have lived what I said. Undefiled by sin from now on, I wish to lead you further in love. Abandon your hearts to me! Thank you for having responded to my call (December 26, 1985).*

Throughout 1985, Mary talked about love in twenty messages. That means she spoke about love almost every other week. At the end of the year, she gives thanks for our obedience to her messages and expresses her desire to lead those who belong to her (and all belong to her) further into love. This is a mother's word of thanksgiving, but it also teaches us to decide to go further. We should continue to grow in love, to overcome sin, and not allow ourselves to be stained by evil nor allow divisions or anything that would destroy life. This must be a continuous effort which we should undertake.

There is not a single day which is not a gift from God. There is not a single day when we cannot do good. There is not a single day when we may not experience failure. But, there is not a single day when we cannot experience the grace of forgiveness. To use every day as if it were the last one, and then again as if it were the first one, is indeed a sign of great maturity. Our human hearts would be enriched with a great inner freedom if we would meet people each time as if we were meeting them for the first time, and treat them as if we are meeting them for the last time.

It is not necessary to carry burdens from the past because love can take them away. But we should not burden ourselves with a fear of future days either. Because, where there is love there is neither fear nor anxiety. Where there is love, there is also abandonment. To accomplish one task and begin another with complete surrender to the will of God and to Mary is a good ending and an even better beginning.

"Thank you, Mary, for the messages through which you love as a mother and have talked about love. Help us to be good students in your school. Teach us to listen with love and, from day to day, to become more beautiful, dressed in the garment of goodness, gentleness, humbleness and love. Help us so that nothing can tear the garment of peace. Mother, we consecrate ourselves to you. Lead us to the eternal love which has made you our most beautiful and dearest Mother. Amen."

Take care, brothers, that none of you have an evil and unfaithful heart, thereby forsaking the living God. Encourage yourselves daily while it is still "today," so that none of you grow hardened by the deceit of sin. We have become partners of

Christ only if we maintain to the end that confi-
dence with which we began. When Scripture says,
"Oh, that today you would hear His voice, harden
not your hearts as at the rebellion" (Heb. 3:12-15).

* * * * * * *

TO BELIEVE in the MOTHER'S LOVE

Dear Children! Today also I am calling you to
prayer. Your prayers are necessary to me so that
God may be glorified through all of you. Dear
children, I pray you, obey and live the Mother's
invitation, because only out of love am I calling
you in order that I might help you. Thank you
for having responded to my call (January 16,
1986).

Our human experience tells us and reminds us that our
actions, our efforts, and even our love toward others and
toward God, are efforts for our own gain. What we seek
is recognition, a response to love, respect from others and
praise. On a human level we can understand and justify
this. But we have to admit, however, that even our acts
of love are clouded by selfishness, personal advancement
and a desire for self-glory and sometimes by desires to control and to be in control. There is probably no other way
on the human level, but, by divine love, our actions can
become free from our personal intentions, and be more
purified.

This kind of gift giving makes us happy, even when our
life is in question. He who expects immediate payment,
reward, success, or recognition will be a burden to himself
because he has to succeed and be recognized, and to others
because others are expected, either out of regard, or out of
fear, to give praises. This kind of person is like a beggar or
hired worker who runs after daily success or daily reward.
At that point a person can either free himself so that whatever he does gives glory to God, or he can enslave and bind

himself in his actions, looking at everything through his own glasses and never being happy or satisfied. God glorifies Himself through those who continuously cooperate with Him and who continuously serve in humility.

Mary calls us to prayer. Through prayer we can cleanse ourselves, because prayer is meeting God. In prayer a person learns to yield to God and to others. Without prayer it is impossible to realize true Christian love. Without prayer we are always in danger of taking over what does not belong to us, thus overshadowing the glory of God and torturing those around us.

Mary's role is to teach us how to love God and other people correctly. Through prayer we receive strength to do that which we recognize as good. If we notice that we are not advancing spiritually, then that is a sign that we are not praying enough. Let us begin to pray for the Lord to purify our intentions!

> *So whenever you eat or drink, or whatever you do, do everything for the glory of God. Avoid giving offense, whether to Jew or Greek or the church of God, just as I try to please everyone in every way, not seeking my own benefit but that of the many, that they may be saved (1 Cor. 10:31-33).*

* * * * * * *

WHEN YOU HELP, DO IT with LOVE

> *Dear Children! Today I call you to live Lent by means of your little sacrifices. Thank you for every sacrifice you have offered to me. Dear children, continue to live in this way and with your love help me to offer sacrifice. God will reward you for that. Thank you for having responded to my call (March 13, 1986).*

The one who loves is ready to do everything possible, on

every occasion, for another. These actions, when they become hard or when a person risks his life or his material goods, are called sacrifices, even though we should not always connect sacrifice with something difficult or unpleasant. That depends on love. Lent is the time when Christ should be before the Christian constantly as the One Who gives His life, Who carries the cross and Who dies on the cross. All this has become a great testimony of His love. This we call His sacrifice for us. His love, which is confirmed by sacrifice, is indeed an inspiration to those who believe in Him and love Him.

Mary leads us to Jesus. She cannot, in any way, bypass Christ Who suffered and with Whom she suffered. Through her love, she showed what a great sacrifice she was ready to offer for Him and with Him. Lent is a time of conversion, a time for abandoning selfishness and conceit, along with other evils and sins. Lent is a time to be inspired with a new love for the Christian ideals which are worth giving everything for, together with Christ. The condition for understanding this is, indeed, our looking at Christ. One who stands aside and is not ready to give of his time or his goods, to give of himself, truly remains on the side and is not overtaken with the new spirit which should be born in Lent.

Therefore, Mary, our Mother, calls us to practice penance and she promises a reward which God prepares for those who offer sacrifices with love. Mary knows that it is easier for us to understand love and sacrifice when we know that we will receive something, when we think of a reward. The greatest reward is to be able to love God above all, to love ourselves correctly, and to love our neighbor as ourselves. One thing that everyone should notice and remember is that Mary gives thanks for sacrifices and for love. The reason for her thanksgiving is not so much in what we do for her, but rather, that we help her to do things for us. The facts are obvious; with love and sacrifice we help ourselves to mature as humans and as Christians, as children of God who are growing in the image which is engraved in our hearts.

Blessed be the God and Father of Our Lord Jesus Christ, the Father of compassion and God of all encouragement, who encourages us in our every affliction, so that we may be able to encourage those who are in any affliction, with the encouragement with which we ourselves are encouraged by God. For as Christ's sufferings overflow to us, so through Christ does our encouragement also overflow (2 Cor. 1:3-5).

*   *   *   *   *   *   *

THE GREATEST SACRIFICE IS LOVE

Dear Children! I wish to thank you for all the sacrifices and I invite you to the greatest sacrifice, the sacrifice of love. Without love, you are not able to accept either me or my Son. Without love, you cannot talk of your experiences to others. Therefore, dear children, I call you to begin to live love within yourselves. Thank you for having responded to my call (March 27, 1986).

Lent is a call to life through a new covenant, the covenant of love. On March 13, just two weeks previously, Our Lady recommended that we do everything with love and that we help with love. She encouraged all in the beginning of Lent to perform sacrifices, penances and fasting with love, so that they would have their full value. In this message the surprise words are "the greatest sacrifice is **love**." Obviously, it is necessary to change our way of thinking in order to comprehend this message. Sacrifice is always hard for us. When we die to ourselves and to our own wants, and so give more of ourselves to others and to God, it can be something unpleasant. For as much as the word "sacrifice" seems unpleasant in our everyday language, every time we hear that someone is sacrificing himself for us, we feel a sense of gratitude, love, joy and security. The sacrifice of others for us opens us up to the value of life. It is a testament of love for us.

How can love be the greatest **sacrifice,** when love makes a person happy, makes our suffering easy and makes every life happy? Somewhere at the end of our contemplations and feelings, at our conclusions and understanding, sacrifice becomes love, and love becomes the greatest sacrifice. One who does not love, cannot sacrifice. One who does not sacrifice, does not grow in love. When a person grows in love, sacrifice becomes an expression of greatest love; and greatest love leads to sacrifice.

Our Lady lived with Jesus. She is His mother and teacher. She lived with Him, learning with Him the greatest sacrifice, the sacrifice of love. As she cannot accept Jesus without love, so she knows that we could not accept Jesus without grace and love. Our experience, our testimony to love, becomes a light, a way and a truth to others. To begin to renew love within ourself means to transform everything into a sacrifice of love. Sacrifice leads us out of sin and death and so gives us life.

Beloved, let us love one another, because love is of God; everyone who loves is begotten by God and knows God. Whoever is without love does not know God, for God is love. In this way the love of God was revealed to us: God sent His only Son into the world so that we might have life through Him. In this is love: not that we have loved God, but that He loved us and sent His Son as expiation for our sins (1 Jn. 4:7-10).

* * * * * * *

LOVE IS the KEY to ENTER the MYSTERY

Dear Children! I wish to call you to a living of the Holy Mass. There are many of you who have sensed the beauty of the Holy Mass, but there are also those who come without joy. I have chosen you, dear children, and Jesus gives you His graces in the Mass. Therefore, consciously live the Holy Mass and let your coming to it be a joyful one. Come to it with love and make the Mass your own. Thank you for having responded to my call (April 3, 1986).

The Sacrifice which truly saves the world is Holy Mass. Love brings the sacrifice of love, of the first Good Friday, to our day and makes it alive among us. Love is what compelled Christ to remain with us. His almighty, divine love transforms bread and wine into the divine sacrifice for the salvation of mankind. Christ's eucharistic love gives itself as a gift in the Holy Sacrifice of the Mass. It is this love which, in a special way, deserves our response. Through love, we come with love, to accept the Mass and to be thankful for the continuous act of Christ's love which is sacrificing itself. But, only our coming with love can lead us into the mystery of this immeasurable divine love which is so concretely and so simply giving itself.

Mary's mission is, indeed, to educate us, so that we can meet Christ in Eucharistic Love. We need to pray for this gift of eucharistic love. Then we would always, with enormous joy, come to Mass and partake and be immersed into the mystery of this love. Mary wants us to understand that the Mass is the act in which Jesus always dies for us, in order that we may live. Each one of us can freely say, "Now He is dying for me. In His death my mortality is being destroyed and the gate of life is opening for me."

This, however, cannot be expressed by words. Indeed, words would not be of any use, just as it would not be of any use to simply describe fresh water to someone who is thirsty. Love is the key by which we open the mystery of divine love and which penetrates our heart and soul, so that we will become able to respond to this love with our whole being: to become the heavenly bread through our thoughts, words, and deeds for all people, and to keep dying and resurrecting with others and for others.

This is my commandment: love one another as I love you. No one has greater love than this, to lay down one's life for one's friends. You are My

*friends if you do what I command you...It is not
you who chose me, but I who chose you and
appointed you to go and bear fruit that will
remain... (Jn. 15:12-14). This is my body which
will be given up for you...This is my blood, which
will be shed for you (Lk. 22:19,20).*

*　*　*　*　*　*　*

TO GROW in LOVE

*Dear Children! I desire to call you to grow in
love. A flower is not able to grow normally without water. So also you, dear children, are not able
to grow without God's blessing. From day to day
you need to seek His blessing so you will grow normally and perform all your actions in union with
God. Thank you for having responded to my call*
(April 10, 1986).

Love is a grace. But it is also the fruit of our cooperation
with that grace. Mary is a mother and, therefore, always in
a simple, visual, but wise and deep way, she educates and
explains. Each seed is a gift. But to become a flower it needs
sun, fertile ground, water, and constant care by human
hands. Only when all these conditions are met does the seed
grow and develop in a natural way.

So it is with love. Love is a divine seed in our hearts. God
loved us before we were created. He loved us at the thought
of our existence. He loved us when no one was able to
imagine, or know, that He would create us. His love led us
out of eternal nothingness and left deep marks in our hearts,
but it remained as a seed. That is why we have an innate,
deep desire for love. It brings within itself the law of development which can be compared with the development of a seed
into a flower and maturing into a fruit. Sun, for the development of our love, is God's blessing, God's grace. As the seed
needs the sun every day so we need the gift of divine love.
For us, that is the law of life.

Many people's lives are like dried branches, or dried-out trees. For other people, the love of God never starts to grow. So, they remain as seeds, cluttered with sin and with the evils of the world. Therefore, the struggle against sin is, at the same time, the struggle for life. Mary, as Mother of love and Mother of life, calls us to grow in love because it means that her motherly role is being realized. To answer the call, to seek God's blessing, to cooperate with grace, to work with God and in God is our expected response! Let us do this out of love for ourselves. Let us extend our hand today. One thing is certain, it is not yet too late!

> *Hear this! A sower went out to sow. And as he sowed, some seed fell on the path, and the birds came and ate it up. Other seed fell on rocky ground where it had little soil. It sprang up at once, because the soil was not deep. And when the sun rose, it was scorched and it withered for lack of roots. Some seed fell among thorns, and the thorns grew up and choked it and it produced no grain. And some seed fell on rich soil and produced fruit. It came up and grew and yielded thirty, sixty and a hundredfold (Mk. 4:3-9).*

*   *   *   *   *   *   *

WITH LOVE into RESPONSIBILITY

> *Dear Children! You are the ones responsible for the messages. The source of grace is here, but you, dear children, are the vessels which transport the gifts. Therefore, dear children, I am calling you to do your job with responsibility. Each one shall be responsible according to his own ability. Dear children, I am calling you to give the gifts to others with love, and not to keep them for yourselves. Thank you for having responded to my call (May 8, 1986).*

Our Lady's presence, and her messages, are great gifts. God's love for us in this world is being revealed these days by sending us Mary, the Mother. Wherever she comes, new places open up where the people of God find springs of love, light, and peace. New unions are being created, the Church is renewing itself and the world is being healed. When individuals open themselves up personally, then darkness disappears from their life and so do sin and death.

Throughout the history of the world, God has been giving such places as gifts to His people. It is at these Marian shrines across the world that Mary gathers millions of her children. This is true of her apparitions in Medjugorje. Multitudes of individuals have begun to live a new life and have been healed spiritually, mentally, and physically. The number of these people is growing. Sin and evil have wounded their hearts, and God, through Mary, has given them the gift of healing.

Mary speaks about the springs of grace. She also speaks about us as vessels which carry these gifts of grace to others. Therefore, the healing of the soul and body, especially spiritual healing, is not only a gift given to the individual person, but then through Him, as through a healthy vessel, it is given to others. Every gift carries with it a responsibility. It cannot be hidden. If it were to be hidden, it would disappear, it would suffocate. By extending a gift it grows and matures. Therefore, when Our Lady talks about responsibility for the messages and when she invites us to extend them to others with love, she is not only concerned about others, who need to learn about the gifts we received from God, but she also thinks of us. Because by experiencing the gift, we live by it and in living it, we help others to understand God's love.

It is a joyful fact that many pilgrims who returned from Medjugorje became true apostles of the message of peace. They have organized many prayer groups and they have become involved in humanitarian actions, especially in saving the unborn life. They respond to a religious lifestyle, giving a clear witness that they received the grace through Our Lady, and for that they testify all their life. There have been incidents in which people who were far from Church and any kind of religious life have come to Medjugorje unplanned, and they return to their communities as living witnesses. Their friends are surprised by their change and they soon begin to share in the spirit of prayer and peace. This is Our Lady's desire for all parishioners and for all pilgrims, for every Christian.

> *Yet preaching the gospel is not the subject of a boast; I am under compulsion and have no choice. I am ruined if I do not preach it! If I do it willingly, I have my recompense; if unwillingly, I am nonetheless entrusted with a charge (1 Cor. 9:16-17).*

*   *   *   *   *   *   *

I AM GIVING YOU MY LOVE

> *Dear Children! Today I wish to give you my own love. You do not know, dear children, how great my love is, and you do not know how to accept it. In various ways I wish to show it to you, but you, dear children, do not recognize it. You do not understand my words with your heart and neither are you able to comprehend my love. Dear children, accept me in your life and so you will be able to accept all I am saying to you and to which I am calling you. Thank you for having responded to my call (May 22, 1986).*

Love is the most beautiful gift that we can give to anyone. Love is the greatest gift. Whatever we give to others, or whatever others give to us, if it is given without love, it seems to lose some value. When we receive human love, our heart lives and blossoms. What joy, then, should our human hearts feel when we hear the joyful news that God is giving us His love, Mary. She also wants to give us her love as a gift. Mary's love is resourceful and finds ways of opening the eyes of those she loves, so that we can see and accept love. The first response to love is that it be accepted and not rejected.

54

Only then can we effectively respond and discover love.

However, in this message Our Lady complains—as a mother who loves. We the people, her children, are not recognizing her love. Our hearts are closed, our eyes blinded, and our ears deaf. What is happening with people today? Many do not recognize love anymore and are not able to accept love. This is the description of a terrible diagnosis for spiritual death! What great sadness Our Lady must feel when she sees her children in such condition! Her sadness is as great as is her love. How hard it would be for a mother if her own children do not recognize her or if their hearts are not open to her.

So today's man is in a strange situation; the farther he is from love, the more he desires it. Unfulfilled desire disappoints and closes the heart, and man becomes more unhappy. This is the circle of death in which many people are entangled. God, in His love, is not forgetting the world and He is offering Himself through Mary.

I am convinced that there is nothing left for us but to pray that we can recognize and accept Our Lady's love and God's love with our heart. Then we will be able to accept with love all of her messages and everything that she wants to give us. It is very difficult to see blindness in those whom you regard as your own. When those we love close their eyes to us, it offends us the most; but when they are open to our love, we are joyful.

> *He was in the world, and the world came to be through Him, but the world did not know Him. He came to what was His own, but His own people did not accept Him. But to those who did accept Him, He gave power to become children of God (Jn. 1:10-12).*

* * * * * * *

LOVE with an ARDENT LOVE

Dear Children! Today my call to you is that in your life you live love toward God and neighbor. Without love, dear children, you can do nothing. Therefore, dear children, I am calling you to live in mutual love. Only in that way will you be able to love and accept both me and all those around you who are coming into your parish. Everyone will sense my love through you. Therefore, I beseech you, dear children, to start loving from today with an ardent love, the love with which I love you. Thank you for having responded to my call (May 29, 1986).

Spoken words have their effects. With words we console, advise, encourage, trust, and ask forgiveness. We can freely say that every person, each one of us, is the word. The closer the word is to us the more it comes from deep within our being and the more it resembles us. God is Word. And that Word is God, because the Word expresses the essence of God. A person is word. The question remains only, how much is a person connected to his word.

A nice word brings out something nice, but it can also bring great danger in itself. If a nice word is not confirmed in deeds or in our conduct, then it becomes a sword with two blades. This is especially true of the word *love*. To talk about love, and not to love, leaves wounds and disappointments. It causes revenge and stirs up a need for aggression. But when the word *love* is confirmed by actions, peace always results.

Mary presents herself as a *Mother* in the above message. She places in our hands a key which can unlock human hearts. If we do not accept this key, we will not be able to achieve much in our lives. And if we accept it ardently, then everything becomes possible. But, love has it's laws. It is necessary to love ourselves and the people around us, all people, without exception. If we do not love our "neighbor" we cannot love God. To make it clear, we could say if we do not take the first step, we cannot take a second one either, and especially not a third one.

Love of God is closely connected with mutual love. We can love God because we love our neighbor. And we love our neighbors with the gift of divine love. This is the great desire of Our Lady. She knows that pilgrims, her dear children, will come and she wants to educate the parish to accept them with the same love with which she loves them. Just how much we in the parish still have to grow in love we probably do not understand. But we can pray more. To let ourselves be loved is a great grace. To be able to love even those who do not want to be loved is the responbility of Christian love.

It is only right that I should entertain such expectations in your regard since I hold all of you dear—you who, to a man, are sharers of my gracious lot when I lie in prison or am summoned to defend the solid grounds on which the Gospel rests. God Himself can testify how much I long for each of you with the affection of Jesus Christ! My prayer is that your love may more and more abound, both in understanding and wealth of experience, so that with a clear conscience and blameless conduct you may learn to value the things that really matter, up to the very day of Christ Jesus. It is my wish that you may be found rich in the harvest of justice which Jesus Christ has ripened in you, to the glory and praise of God (Phil. 1:7-11).

*   *   *   *   *   *   *

LOVE, the VICTORY OVER SIN and HARDSHIP

Dear Children! Today I am calling you to holiness. Without holiness you cannot live. Therefore, with love overcome every sin and with love overcome all the difficulties which are coming to you. Dear children, I beseech to you to live love within yourselves. Thank you for having responded to my call (July 10, 1986).

Sin is a reality of our lives and of this world. It is a dark, opposing force, a destructive action in the world. To conquer sin means to advance constantly in building up our lives, the lives of others, our families, communities, society, the Church, and the world. To conquer sin would mean that not a single just wish would be suffocated, and not a single cry would fall on deaf ears, not a single tear would fall into the dark abyss of hopelessness, nor a single hope would be betrayed.

How to create a new person, a happier family, a more just society is the question which is being put forth to all religions, indeed, to the whole world. Many answers are proposed, solutions are offered, things are being discussed and promised, but the world, from day to day, suffers more pain, more aggression and greater injustice. Who knows when the world will come close to that which, deep within, it desires and yearns for.

Mary also, as a sign of a better world and confirmation of a promise given by God, touches upon the same question and gives an answer. With love you can overcome evil and sin. With love you can move forward. Love even heals that which is wounded by sin. Therefore, we can say that love is a constant inspiration for good. Love offers an unbeatable power to fight against hardship and transforms everything to good for the building up and the salvation of the world. Love gives the power which is unreachable by normal human means. Love, which is poured by God into the hearts of people, is the power which mankind yearns for to overcome all the crises to which it is subjected.

It is necessary to pray daily so that the world will open up to this divine love and save itself through it. We Christians are in danger of committing a great injustice to the world if we do not reveal this divine love to the world. Mary, therefore, says, *I beg you to realize love in yourself.*

> *So, gird the loins of your understanding; live soberly; set all your hope on the gift to be conferred on you when Jesus Christ appears. As obedient sons, do not yield to the desires that once shaped you in your ignorance. Rather, become holy in yourselves in every aspect of your conduct, after the likeness of the Holy One Who called you; remember, Scripture says, "Be holy, for I am holy" (1 Pt. 1:13-16).*

*   *   *   *   *   *   *

REALIZE LIFE THROUGH LOVE

> *Dear Children! Today I am calling you to reflect upon why I am with you this long. I am the Mediatrix between you and God. Therefore, dear children, I desire to call you to live always out of love all that which God desires of you. For that reason, dear children, in your own humility live all the messages which I am giving you. Thank you for having responded to my call* (July 17, 1986).

Life is a gift. This, indeed, is true for every life. It is true even for a life which we personally might think makes no sense. The gift-giver of life is God Himself Who, in His wisdom, distributes all things and guides them to their fullness. It is often impossible for us to recognize this fullness during our earthly sojourn. We might not recognize the purpose of life and we might have a problem with those who are ill or who do not have the physical, mental, or spiritual capacity to grow. The measures by which we evaluate the purpose of life could be our obstacle. However, the fact that we exist, that we have been created, implies that our life and every life has its deep meaning and it is possible to realize its fullness.

Mary is calling us and she reminds us that God has His plan for everyone. God desires that we live according to His plan. His plan is deeply carved in our souls and hearts and we can know it and realize it. A person receives peace by following God's will. Mary experienced freedom and freely decided for God's plan. She knows that our personal freedom can endanger God's plan for us. She is staying with us at this time because she can intercede and help us as a mother. When she asks us humbly to accept her call, she calls us to the conduct which we, who are God's creatures, should have before God.

Humility is not degrading to a human being, but rather it is a call to accept cooperation with God who has His plan for us. In God's plan, Mary experienced how important it is to give complete acceptance and to believe that everything is possible to God. We suffocate God's plan for us when we do not obey and do not accept humbly what God offers us. It is always disadvantageous to the spiritual life of our soul to remain in the old, sinful, material, possessive condition. It is of enormous value for us to accept and to be grateful for Mary's intercession.

And now, brothers, I beg you through the mercy of God to offer your bodies as a living sacrifice holy and acceptable to God, your spiritual worship. Do not conform yourselves to this age, but be transformed by the renewal of your mind, so that you may judge what is God's will, what is good, pleasing, and perfect (Rom. 12:1-2).

* * * * * * *

WITH LOVE TRANSFORM EVERYTHING to GOOD

Dear Children! Hatred gives birth to dissensions and does not regard anyone or anything. I call you always to begin harmony and peace. Especially, dear children, in the place where you live, do everything with love. Let your only instrument always be love. By love turn everything into good which Satan desires to destroy and possess. Only that way shall you be completely mine and I shall be able to help you. Thank you for having responded to my call (July 31, 1986).

What a great promise Our Lady offers—*to turn everything to good;* all hardship, all suffering, all pain. Human hearts eagerly listen to those words with joy because they concern one of the eternal questions which troubles humanity.

I believe that we have to recognize the fact that the mystery of evil and the mystery of suffering remains unsolvable to human reasoning. However, "to turn everything to good" is not a condition for understanding everything. Therefore, we can believe that love is the mysterious key which heals all wounds caused by hate. Love is a saving medicine which heals and corrects what has been destroyed in a person's vision and the person sees again. In other words, as hate turns everything to evil, destroying, separating, blinding, hardening the human heart, turning human hands into iron hands and turning every step into a criminal step, so love heals and transforms everything into good.

Mary, as Mother, cares about each of us, our families and the whole world. She rejoices as a mother in the successes of her children, because they are also her successes. But she also becomes sad when she sees the failures and the destruction people are causing themselves. She is "a woman clothed with the sun, with the moon under her feet," in constant battle with Satan the instigator of hate and division. That is the reason she calls us to unity and peace, for that is the opposite action, the saving, reconciling action. With love we build peace in an unpeaceful world. We bring justice to a world of injustice, mercy to a world of rudeness, light to a world in darkness, and life to a world of death. We should act with love in the family, the work place, the school, the community, and the Church. Love should be the means in our hands through which we build the world.

Mary is calling us to this. She is calling us to abandon all other means which do not lead to good. She calls us to decide to be hers totally, living in love and conquering Satan and everything that comes from him, and so to be worthy of our Mother.

> *The Spirit too helps us in our weakness, for we do not know how to pray as we ought; but the Spirit Himself makes intercession for us with groaning which cannot be expressed in speech. He who searches hearts knows what the Spirit means, for the Spirit intercedes for the saints as God Himself will (Rom. 8:26-27).*

* * * * * * *

UNDERSTAND the IMMEASURABLE LOVE

> *Dear Children! I thank you for the love which you are showing me. You know, dear children, that I love you immeasurably and daily I pray the Lord to help you to understand the love which I am showing you. Therefore, you, dear children, pray, pray, pray! Thank you for having responded to my call (August 21, 1986).*

Thankfulness is an excellent virtue. To know how to say "thank you" means to accept others and to recognize their value for us personally, as well as for others. Thanksgiving is the connection between people through which we build and strengthen mutual relationships and through which we rebuild broken bridges. The words "thank you" make the one who speaks, and the one to whom we speak, happy. In a special way, thanksgiving brings joy when it exceeds the barriers of "politeness" and responds to the true state of being. This means that before we give thanks for something which has been done for us, we are able to give thanks for the gift of the "person." When we begin to feel joy for the presence of others and begin to give thanks for them, and others do the same for us, then life becomes joy and peace. This is a mother's joy for her child who is joyfully accepted.

Our Lady gives thanks for our love, and by this she offers a condition for our happiness and peace. She responds with an immeasurable love which surpasses human concepts and understanding. To understand with the heart that we are loved means to find a way to the deepest happiness. This means, in reality, to be in paradise. Paradise is, in a sense, nothing more than being loved and responding with love, and constantly experiencing joy for the presence of others and giving thanks for their existence.

Whether we are happy or not matters to Our Lady and she wants to educate us for this happiness. We cannot expect happiness to be something which will be dropped in our lap, but happiness is something for which we have to intercede personally. Our Lady prays to the Lord, who loves us unconditionally, that we can understand His love, the love which He is showing through Mary. She is beseeching us with a three-fold call to pray that this may happen.

> *We keep thanking God for all of you and we remember you in our prayers, for we constantly are mindful before our God and Father of the way you are proving your faith, and laboring in love, and showing constancy of hope in our Lord Jesus Christ. We know, too, brothers, beloved of God, how you were chosen. Our preaching of the Gospel provided not a mere matter of words for you but one of power; it was carried on in the Holy Spirit and out of complete conviction. . . (1 Thes. 1:2-4, 5a).*

*   *   *   *   *   *   *

ACCEPT SUFFERING with LOVE

Dear Children! For these days while you are joyfully celebrating the cross, I desire that your cross also would be a joy for you. Especially, dear children, pray that you may be able to accept sickness and suffering with love the way Jesus accepted them. Only that way shall I be able with joy to give out to you the graces and healings which Jesus is permitting me. Thank you for having responded to my call (September 11, 1986).

Suffering remains a mystery even when we meditate upon it in front of Our Lord's Cross. There remains a question and a constant mystery even though we joyfully celebrate the Cross and sing victorious songs. In its mystery, the Cross for the Christian is a sign of victory, but for others, it is a scandal and a shame. Illness and suffering are crosses which can easily close the human heart to God, and temporarily distance ourselves from God. We ask, "Why, O God?" However, it is generally true that the experience of personal or family suffering usually brings fruits of faith, love, and hope.

Jesus asked a similar question in the Garden of Gethsemane and He did not receive an answer. But an angel encouraged Him when He accepted the Father's will. Instead of questioning God, "Where are You?" we can ask ourselves, our family, our Church, and all mankind, "Where are we?" Much suffering comes from the fact that we do not convert, do not love, do not forgive, and do not reconcile. This is why wars and many other destructions happen. We also have the innocent who suffer in the name of others and for others. And so, there is suffering because we do not love, and there is suffering because we do love.

Mary courageously invites us to accept the Cross with love. As an example, she points to her Son, Jesus, whom she witnessed as He carried His Cross and endured His suffering. She tells us how we can carry our crosses. She did not say, *Carry your cross,* because she knows we are weak. Instead she said, *Pray that you can accept illness and suffering with love.* We usually pray that the Lord lifts our suffering and crosses and this is understandable. But we have to accept the fact that we need to pray to be able to accept our crosses and suffering with love. Because, in the light of Christ's Cross, suffering is given an important place, not as a curse or scandal, but rather as the way towards life.

I consider the sufferings of the present to be as nothing compared with the glory to be revealed in us. Indeed, the whole created world eagerly awaits the revelation of the sons of God. Creation was made subject to futility, not of its own accord but by Him who once subjected it; yet not without hope, because the world itself will be freed from its slavery to corruption and share in the glorious freedom of the children of God (Rom. 8:18-21).

* * * * * * *

DEVOTION to PRAYER with LOVE

Dear Children! Today again I am calling you to pray. You, dear children, are not able to understand how great the value of prayer is as long as you yourselves do not say: 'Now is the time for prayer, now nothing else is important to me, now not one person is important to me but God.' Dear children, consecrate yourselves to prayer with a special love so that God will be able to render graces back to you. Thank you for having responded to my call (October 2, 1986).

Prayer is an expression of our relationship with God. Therefore, a problem with prayer always reflects a problem with this relationship. One who loves God will pray with ease, and will pray more. One who loves God will commit himself to prayer with love. The more we spend time with the Lord in prayer, the more we will love Him. Then we will have more time for prayer. In this way, our life is transformed into prayer.

By growing in love toward God, everything we do helps us to keep meeting Him and to be in touch with Him. It will not be hard to find the time, a place, and the people to pray with. Therefore, we can say that all those who think they have a problem with prayer really only have a problem with their relationship with God. This does not mean that we cannot use different forms of prayer at different times, but every form of prayer should be an expression of love towards God.

How do we start to pray? What is the difference between the decision to pray and praying with love? These are questions which naturally evolve. The beginning of the answer to these questions can be found within the human heart. Prayer, like love, is given to us as a gift, as a seed which needs to be taken care of to enable it to grow and to develop. This care of prayer should come as naturally as a child learns to speak with its mother's language. However, in this world life is not so natural that the gift of prayer can be naturally developed. That is the reason why God raises special people, communities, or places where, in a special way, a desire for prayer can be awakened and accepted by people. That place for many in recent years has been Medjugorje, and the Queen of Peace.

The spirit of prayer was awakened by the visionaries in Medjugorje and the places of prayer are the Hill of Apparitions, Cross Mountain, and the parish Church. This awakened desire for God seeks order and regularity. It seeks a commitment; a commitment with love. When we begin to pray, we need consciously to leave everything else behind, all work and all people. It is necessary to turn off the television and not respond to the telephone and find a quiet corner in our home in which to pray. This will help us meet God within ourselves. Very often we allow things, people, and events to pull us away from prayer. Mary, the teacher of spiritual life, seeks from us a concrete and lasting decision to pray and she promises success.

Stop worrying, then, over questions like, "What are we to eat, what are we to drink, or what are we to wear?" The unbelievers are always running after these things. Your heavenly Father knows all that you need. Seek first His kingship over you, His way of holiness, and all these things will be given you besides. Enough then of worrying about tomorrow. Let tomorrow take care of itself. Today has enough troubles of its own (Matt. 6:31-34).

* * * * * * *

HOLINESS in FREEDOM and LOVE

Dear Children! You know that I desire to lead you on the way of holiness, but I do not want to compel you to be saints by force. I desire that each of you by your own little self-denials help yourself and me so I can lead you from day to day closer to holiness. Therefore, dear children, I do not desire to force you to observe the messages. But rather this long time that I am with you is a sign that I love you immeasurably and what I desire of each individual is to become holy. Thank you for having responded to my call (October 9, 1986).

Faith is an act of the reason and of the heart. Love is an act of the heart and a product of the heart and reason. Therefore, no one can be forced either to love or to have faith. The fact remains, however, that every person must have faith in something in order to live, and everyone needs to be loved in order to endure life. Freedom is a gift of God. By giving us freedom, we could say that God limited His Almightiness and conditioned it by human freedom. So then, those who accept love and faith in freedom begin on the path of holiness.

Holiness means, first of all, an inner, spiritual healing from sin and its consequences, and a constant growing into the image of God. The one who grows toward the plan which God has impressed on His heart becomes holy. Man can resist this plan, but this spiritual growth will stop. Man brings damage and evil on himself when he resists the call to holiness. Since it is part of his very nature, it remains a mystery why a person does not immediately accept, and with enthusiasm, the call to holiness.

Mary is holy. She was conceived without sin and, with the power of grace by her cooperation with mercy, she accomplished complete holiness because God's will was fully realized in her life. She wants us to follow the path of inner freedom from sin which is the first step towards holiness. Small denials, sufferings, and struggles are important until we begin taking bigger steps toward the deepness of God's love. Then the love of God becomes the main motivator of the human force on the path to holiness, because holiness means walking closer to God.

Mary stays with us through her apparitions because she loves us. She does not force us because she does not want slaves, but free children. Her love is such that she leaves it to us to pray daily so that we may become holy. While she is calling us to denials and to the way of holiness, it seems that in her deep concern for our freedom, she is apologizing, saying that she does not want anything by force. May her immeasurable love find more and more hearts which are ready to respond.

> *But to attain this, you will have to do your utmost yourselves, adding goodness to the faith that you have, understanding to your goodness, self-control to your understanding, patience to your self-control, true devotion to your patience, kindness towards your fellow men to your devotion, and, to this kindness, love. If you have a generous supply of these, they will not leave you ineffectual or unproductive. They will bring you to a real knowledge of our Lord Jesus Christ. But without them a man is blind or else short-sighted; he has forgotten how his past sins were washed away (2 Pt. 1:5-9).*

*   *   *   *   *   *   *

TO ACCEPT with LOVE

Dear Children! Today again I desire to call you to take seriously and carry out the messages which I am giving you. Dear children, it is for your sake that I have stayed this long so I could help you to fulfill all the messages which I am giving you. Therefore, dear children, out of love for me carry out all the messages which I am giving you. Thank you for having responded to my call (October 30, 1986).

The messages that our Lady is giving us are evangelical messages, spoken in a simple, motherly way. Everything that is happening around and with these messages is obvious proof of her motherly love and wisdom. For all those who have accepted Medjugorje, the first message is Mary herself, the mother who is present and who is calling. This has always been the first reason why the pilgrims come, even if it is not always understood. No one comes to Medjugorje just because the Rosary is prayed here, but because Our Lady is appearing here. When the pilgrims come they also hear our other messages—reconcile, convert, pray, fast, believe, participate in the Holy Mass with love, go to confession once a month, read the Holy Scripture, become holy, abandon yourselves to God, love one another ardently, and be a witness for God to others with love.

Our Lady desires that we seriously accept all of the messages and that we live them. She brings these messages in the name of God and she wants to help us realize them. Here then, is where we find the answer to the often asked question, "Why are the apparitions prolonged?" She wants to help us. That is the answer. Her love has greatly moved many people. It has opened them to divine love and has been the beginning of a new life for many. Her motherly love, and our love toward Our Mother, is a moving power which can change the world. Her providing a consciousness of the Mother whose love sparks peace among people. The happiness and peace of the family depend upon the mother's presence in the family. The same is true of the Church and of the world. For as much as we succeed in bringing, through the conversion of our life, Mary's motherly love into our hearts, our families, our church, and the world, that much will we be successful in bringing peace to our world. Joy and peace, justice and love will meet and embrace only through the Mother's love. A mother's love is not limited to the woman who gives birth to the child, but it spreads to all of those who, by their life, words, and actions, love and guard human freedom and dignity.

How beautiful it would be on earth if people would honor and accept one another with this mother's love! This should be not only our aim but also the way to peace in the world.

This is my commandment: love one another as I love you. No one has greater love than this, to lay down one's life for one's friends. You are my friends if you do what I command you. I no longer call you slaves, because a slave does not know what his master is doing. I have called you friends, because I have told you everything I have heard from my Father. It was not you who chose me, but I who chose you and appointed you to go and bear fruit that will remain, so that whatever you ask the Father in my name He may give you. This I command you: love one another (Jn. 15:12-17).

*   *   *   *   *   *   *

WITH PRAYER to the LOVE of GOD

Dear Children! Today I wish to call you to pray daily for the souls in Purgatory. For every soul prayer and grace is necessary to reach God and the love of God. By doing this, dear children, you obtain new intercessors who will help you in life to realize that all the earthly things are not impor-

tant for you, that only Heaven is that for which it is necessary to strive. Therefore, dear children, pray without ceasing that you may be able to help yourselves and the others to whom your prayers will bring joy. Thank you for having responded to my call (November 6, 1986).

Prayer is an expression of love towards God. So, whoever prays, loves God. Prayer in itself expresses a deep love for God, and a desire to be with Him as with a father whom we love. Prayer is a conversation, a meeting, a union of hearts. However, prayer also has its intercessory power and role. In other words, we Christians can pray for others. We can intercede for them as Mary intercedes for us. Christian ties in themselves are deeper than family ties. So with our prayers we can help others to come to the love of God.

According to Catholic tradition, the pilgrim church can help, by prayers and sacrifices, the suffering church in Purgatory. Souls in Purgatory cannot help themselves but they can intercede for the pilgrim church. In this way, through prayer, a deep connection is formed between the church on earth and the suffering church in Purgatory. Mary is Mother of the Church, the whole Church—glorious, suffering, and pilgrim. She teaches us how we, as her children, can be together and help one another. In these trying times we are losing awareness of this unity which Mary wants to see among her children. Those whom we, the pilgrim church, help to get to Heaven by our prayers and sacrifices become not only helpers and friends but also our teachers. They help us to understand that the things of this world are not important and that only Heaven and eternal life are important.

There is no better mission than a call to help others, to bring them closer to God's love. Meeting up with that love makes us happy and peaceful. Therefore, Mary invites us so that with love we will pray for souls in Purgatory.

The above message was given immediately after the feast of All Saints. Indeed, it is necessary to pay attention to what Our Lady, as Mother, says and to what she is calling us. To help others to come to God's love means to ensure entrance to the same love ourselves.

Whatever gains I had, these I have come to consider a loss because of Christ. More than that, I even consider everything as a loss because of the supreme good of knowing Christ Jesus my Lord. For His sake I have accepted the loss of all things and I consider them so much rubbish, that I may gain Christ and be found in Him, not having any righteousness of my own based on the law but that which comes through faith in Christ, the righteousness from God which depends on faith. I want to know Him and the power of His resurrection and sharing of His sufferings by being conformed to His death, if somehow I may attain the resurrection from the dead (Phil. 3:7-11).

* * * * * * *

GOD'S LOVE and NOT HUMAN LOVE

Dear Children! Today also I am calling you to live and follow with a special love all the messages which I am giving you. Dear children, God does not want you lukewarm and undecided, but that you totally surrender to Him. You know that I love you and that out of love I long for you. Therefore, dear children, you also decide for love so that you will long for and daily experience God's love. Dear children, decide for love so that love prevails in all of you, but not human love, rather God's love. Thank you for having responded to my call (October 20, 1986).

Abandonment to God is necessary if we want to grow in love. Although we always need to keep in mind that love is a grace and a gift, it is necessary continuously and freely to look for that grace. Whoever decides for love will more and more recognize the loved person and begin to burn with love for the person.

The problem with many lovers of today consists in the fact

that their "love" loses with time its abandonment, its flame, its readiness to exist for others. That means that human love tires us. Divine love burns for us. So it is with Mary's love. Therefore, if we are lukewarm and indecisive, we are not worthy of an ardent love which gives itself to us as a gift. The one who is lukewarm and indecisive remains only half way to his destination and gives of himself only partially, incompletely. This incompleteness is especially evident if love towards things leads us astray so that we have no time or place for God.

If our heart yearns more for people and things than it does for God, then something has happened that should not have happened, an exchange which is not worthy of man, the creature of God.

Mary is warning us in this message, with her motherly love, to remain in true love. Divine love is not contrary to human love, but rather insures it. Divine love gives human love foundation and purpose. However, human love, which excludes itself from the lifeline of divine love, easily becomes not only a limitation but an obstacle to divine love. Mary warns us that in all the daily temptations to which our love is subjected we can overcome and emerge as winners, loving God all the more and so growing in human love as well.

The question arises again, "Why does man easily turn his back on that love which is the foundation of his life and turn to a love which destroys him?" Here we see and discover the mystery of sin and the necessity of prayer to the Holy Spirit, so that we will recognize truth and really decide for truth.

Therefore, from the day we heard this, we do not cease praying for you and asking that you may be filled with the knowledge of His will through all spiritual wisdom and understanding. We pray this in order that you may live in a manner worthy of the Lord, so as to be fully pleasing; in every good work bearing fruit and growing in the knowledge of God, strengthened with every power in accord with His glorious might, for all endurance and patience, with joy giving thanks to the Father, who has made you fit to share in the inheritance of the holy ones in light (Col. 1:9-12).

LOVE WANTS ETERNAL UNITY

Dear Children! Again today I call you to conse-crate your life to me with love, so I am able to guide you with love. I love you, dear children, with a special love and I desire to bring you all to Heaven to God. I want you to realize that this life lasts briefly compared to the one in Heaven. Therefore, dear children, decide again today for God. Only that way will I be able to show how much you are dear to me and how much I desire for all to be saved and to be with me in Heaven. Thank you for having responded to my call (November 27, 1986).

The golden rule of every relationship is love. Love cannot be substituted with no rules. Without love, all the rules are only dead letters. They become imposing and improper. We must emphasize that love does not exclude rules, but rather includes rules and regulations which guard love. Love gives them meaning. Every teacher should be devoted to those being taught. And, every student should respond with the same devotion. True devotion means accepting each other with love and it promises constant faithfulness. It also means accepting advice as a gift.

Mary is calling us to consecrate our lives to her. The rea-son is simply that she wants to lead us to Jesus. Only one whom we trust, who loves us, and whom we love, can lead us. There will be less resistance, and even if there is any, it will be transformed to good. It is our human fortune that the love of parents and neighbors grows without our cons-ciously deciding on it. But we should not forget that this love can also be stopped in its development. It depends on parents and the neighbors. It is also fortunate that parental love is given as a gift. A mother loves her child immediately. She is joyful from the moment of conception. There are cases where a mother rejects her child, but unacceptance is a rare reason. Rather, the rejection often results from pressures from spouse, friends, or other circumstances. Love is given as a gift and is the basic relationship between people and the fundamental law of upbringing.

Mary loves us, and with love she wants to lead us into the fullness of love—which is God. To know that we are dear to God is a real and primary condition for life. This love leads us to Heaven, because where there is love there is Heaven. Heaven is an eternal unity in love with God and with one another.

> *But you, man of God, avoid all this. Instead, pursue righteousness, devotion, faith, love, patience, and gentleness. Fight the good fight of the faith. Lay hold of eternal life to which you were called when you make your noble confession in the presence of many witnesses. I charge you before God, who gives life to all things, and before Christ Jesus, who gave testimony under Pontius Pilate for the noble confession to keep the commandment without stain or reproach until the appearance of our Lord Jesus Christ that the blessed and only ruler will make manifest at the proper time, the King of kings and Lord of lords. . . (1 Tim. 6:11-15).*

*   *   *   *   *   *   *

OUT of LOVE TOWARDS GOD and YOU

> *Dear Children! Today I wish to call on all of you that in the New Year you live the messages which I am giving you. Dear children, you know that for your sake I have remained a long time so I might teach you how to make progress on the way of holiness. Therefore, dear children, pray without ceasing and live the messages which I am giving you for I am doing it with great love toward God and toward you. Thank you for having responded to my call* (January 1, 1987).

Mary gave this message at the beginning of a new year, on the day the Church celebrates the feast of her Motherhood. Mary, as a mother, and a wise and good teacher, calls us. She accepts her own as a gift and uses this moment to encourage us. She has given many messages, but if we do not live them they remain dead words. The present moment, this time which is given to us, is the only time that we can count on. There will not be another life on this earth for us. This very day we live, even if it is not the last day, is nevertheless, one day less on earth or one day closer to death and to eternity.

The path in front of us, Mary's children, is *the way of holiness.* This is the way that Mary walked. Pure from sin, she grew in love. She is leading us on the way to holiness, but for us it must first be a way of purification. By purifying ourselves we become holy. By freeing ourselves from evil and darkness, we open ourselves to the good and to the light. While the way is crowned with suffering, it is the way worthy of man. If we do not start on this path, we remain in the evil and are exposed to destruction.

We are consecrated to Mary and she has consecrated herself to us. She consecrated herself to God first and now that consecration becomes her duty for us, a duty which she does out of love toward God. Love of God is always the first responsibility in order that it can turn toward man. Mary is responsible for our development and our advancement is her contribution to the glory of God the Creator. She is tireless because she loves God and us, her children. She does not get discouraged when she is not successful because she believes in God's almighty power which she experienced with her faith. Therefore, our weaknesses and our sins cannot stop her.

A new year for her is not the time to stop trying, but rather a time to offer new encouragement for new efforts. For us personally, a new year should bring a new effort, that with new enthusiasm we will accept the Gospel itself, and with love toward ourselves, toward Mary and toward God, see the new year as a gift and live it as a gift!

May God have pity on us and bless us; may He
let His face shine upon us.

*So may your way be known upon earth; among
all nations, your salvation.*

*May the peoples praise you, O God; may all the
peoples praise you.*

*May the nations be glad and exult because you
rule the peoples in equity; The nations on the
earth you guide.*

*May the peoples praise you, O God; may all the
peoples praise you.*

*The earth has yielded its fruits; God, our God, has
blessed us.*

*May God bless us, and may all the ends of the
earth fear him.*

(Ps. 67:1-8).

* * * * * * *

PERFORM ACTS of LOVE and MERCY

*Dear Children! Today I am grateful to you for
your presence in this place, where I am giving you
special graces. I call each of you to begin to live
as of today that life which God wishes of you and
to begin to perform good works of love and mercy.
I do not want you, dear children, to live the message and be committing sin which is displeasing
to me. Therefore, dear children, I want each of you
to live a new life without destroying all that God
produces in you and is giving you. I give you my
special blessing and I am remaining with you on
your way of conversion. Thank you for having
responded to my call* (March 25, 1987).

Conversion is the way toward new life. New life consists
primarily in freeing oneself from selfishness. Selfishness is
the chain under which the divine seeds of love, faith, and
hope decay in many hearts. Conversion is a beginning in
breaking away from selfishness and the beginning of growing
in love. This is often a painful procedure but the only proce-

dure which pays off. Whoever grows in love, grows to be a person able to be with God and with people as well as with nature itself. The heart which blossoms with love is the most beautiful heart.

Love is fruitful. Acts which are performed with love and which are inspired by love are the acts of mercy. This is indeed a fruit-bearing love. Love is the sharpest eye by which we notice the needs of others. Our love is set into motion and love in motion is resourceful.

This is what Our Lady can wish for us, and from us. Given on the feast of Annunciation the above message has even a deeper meaning. Mary said to God, *May it be done to me according to your word.* By this she performed a great act of mercy. With a merciful heart she allowed God to express His immeasurable love by sending us His Son, to be the Saviour of the world. Mary's consent to the will of God is the beginning of conversion for the human race; a race which, through the sin of our first parents, rejected cooperation with God's will.

The greatest mercy toward ourselves is to allow God to dwell within us as light, as life, love, mercy, and justice. Only then can we turn to others to perform good deeds of love and mercy. Whoever does not renounce sin cannot be merciful toward self. We destroy what God wants to realize in us and Mary is not pleased with this, for she delights in our growth.

Do to others whatever you would have them do to you. This is the law and the prophets (Mt. 7:12).

* * * * * * *

RENEWING GOD'S LOVE and HOLINESS

Dear Children! I am calling everyone of you to start living in God's love. Dear children, you are ready to commit sin, and to put yourselves in the hands of Satan without reflecting. I call on each one of you to decide consciously for God and against Satan. I am your Mother and, therefore, I want to lead you all to perfect holiness. I want each one of you to be happy here on earth and to be with me in Heaven. That is, dear children, the purpose of my coming here and it's my desire. Thank you for having responded to my call (May 25, 1987).

Holiness is another expression for growing in love. In the Roman and Anglo-Saxon languages the word "holiness" has the same root as *sanctum, santa, saint, helix, holy,* words which can help us understand the meaning of holiness. Holiness, first of all, defines the process of healing from sin and its consequences. It helps us conquer temptations and as we grow in holiness we also grow towards the thought and the will of God. No one can grow in holiness if he does not grow in a merciful love toward himself, toward others, toward God, and toward nature. Anyone who resists the process of holiness, who resists God's will and imposes his own will, does not love himself. He cannot love others let alone God.

Holiness is not demonstrated with great deeds, but with doing what we do with a great love. It would be false to think that miracles are special gifts that are given as proof for holiness, even though many holy persons perform great and miraculous deeds. Rather, holiness is a call to resist sin and Satan who wants to stop us on our way. Therefore, every Christian is invited to holiness because holiness is not and cannot be something only for a chosen few.

Our Lady, as holy Mother, knows all this. She wants to guide us to holiness and she wants to bring us up in love toward our own life, toward the life of others, toward everything that is created and finally toward our Creator Himself. From a different point of view, we must decide against death and sin against all satanic action. These are also the conditions for our happiness here on earth and the only way to Heaven. Our Lady is with us, as she tells us, just to guide us in holiness, and this is the reason that she stays so long. As Mother she cannot wish anything else but our growth and development. Only in that way can she be the one who steps on the head of Satan and his descendants, thus opening a free passage to her children. Only then can she be the woman clothed with the sun, with the moon under her feet, when her children are clothed in the garment of holiness.

That we are giving ourselves into the hands of Satan is a heavy word to hear from her. May it be our decision to be holy and to begin to pray each day for this grace.

As for yourself, you must say what is consistent with sound doctrine, namely, that older men should be temperate, dignified, self-controlled, sound in faith, love, and endurance. Similarly, older women should be reverent in their behavior, not slanderers, not addicted to drink, teaching what is good, so that they may train younger women to love their husbands and children, to be self-controlled, chaste, good homemakers, under the control of their husbands, so that the word of God may not be discredited. Urge the younger men, similarly, to control themselves (Titus 2:1-6).

* * * * * * *

THE WAY to GOD IS EASIER with LOVE

Dear Children! Today I want to call all of you to decide for Paradise. The way is difficult for those who have not decided for God. Dear children, decide and believe that God is offering Himself to you in His fullness. You are invited and you need to answer the call of the Father, Who is calling you through me. Pray, because in prayer each one of you will be able to achieve the fullness of love. I am blessing you and I desire to help you so that each one of you might be under my motherly mantle. Thank you for having responded to my call (October 25, 1987).

God is love, therefore, He is offering Himself in His love to His creatures, whom He has gifted with a gift of freedom. God's love, in its essence, desires the response of the human

80

heart, a response of love with love. Love is fulfilled when a connection and unity between loved persons is realized. All of creation and the act of creating are expressions of God's love which is so richly expressed and manifested.

The crown of creation, us, presents the highest expression of God's love. Therefore, we are the most loved of all creatures. Creatures testify to God's love by their existence and we need to accept our existence by our free will in order to become a response to God's love. The decision is free, meaning one has the choice to say yes or no to God. This decision, however, has concrete consequences. If a person, faced with a choice between light and darkness, decides for darkness, then he remains in darkness even though the darkness hinders his life because it is not natural to him. So we, in deciding for or against God, with or without God, make a most important decision. We take fatal steps and we either grow and develop or we destroy ourselves and disappear. In this decision consists the decision for paradise, for Heaven.

Mary's presence among her children becomes God's call for us. God speaks through Mary, in her being and in her response. God calls for peace, giving us signs of forgiveness, signs of His mercy and of His love. Unfortunately, we, His children, have become blind and deaf to His words and His signs. Many people do not even believe that God exists. Or they think that if He exists He is outside of their lives.

In one very simple message in the beginning of the apparitions, Our Lady said, *I came to tell that God exists!* Our Lady wants to pull us out of the ambush. She shows us the way to paradise and to the fullness of life. Her way is full of joy and peace, but hard at the same time. Sin brings out sluggishness, endangering and destroying man's will; but Mary helps us to make a decision so that we can begin decisively toward paradise. Whoever loves himself will decide for this way. Our decision is nourished and our steps empowered with prayer.

Enter through the narrow gate, for the gate is wide and the road broad that leads to destruction, and those who enter through it are many. How narrow the gate and constricted the road that leads to life! And those who find it are few (Mt. 7:13-14).

BELIEVE ME, I LOVE YOU

Dear Children! Today also I call each one of you to decide to surrender again everything completely to me. Only in that way will I be able to present each of you to God. Dear children, you know that I love you immeasurably and that I desire each of you for myself, but God has given to all a freedom which I lovingly respect and humbly submit to. I desire, dear children, that you help so that everything God has planned in this parish shall be realized. If you do not pray, you shall not be able to recognize my love and the plans which God has for this parish and for each individual. Pray that Satan does not entice you with his pride and false power. I am with you and I want you to believe me, that I love you. Thank you for having responded to my call (November 25, 1987).

Whoever loves, honors freedom. The moment we accept freedom, however, love may begin to suffer and be crucified. Love burns with a desire to enrich another person. However, if the other person does not respond, then this desire does not cease but rather waits, offering itself and suffering. It joyfully waits for a moment when it will be able to place a bridge of love over which only the gifts of love can pass. God yearns for His creature, man, but at the same time He waits for a response. Because human love is impatient, changeable, often aggressive, does not honor the freedom of another and is selfish, it needs to be cleansed and it needs to mature.

Our Lady calls us to decide to abandon ourselves to her. She loves us immeasurably. Therefore, she wants each one of us for her own. Her greatest wish is to see us, to teach us, to guide us and to be with us. However, in her humility, she honors our freedom and waits for our response. She is ready to accept even a closed heart and humbly, with love, waits for it to open. Even if some hearts do not open, she continues loving with the same love. Mary treats us the same way God treated her when He sent His angel to ask her if she would accept His divine plan. Her answer was not, *I understand,* but it was, *May it be done to me according to your word!* Abandonment, obedience, humility are the virtues of a free response to love.

Mary warns us that Satan is strong and that he wants to deceive us with his conceit and false pride. He wants to separate us from the plan of God for us as individuals and for the Church. With prayer we can understand God's plan and we will receive grace to accomplish it. With prayer we will receive wisdom to discover Satan's traps and we will receive strength to resist his action.

> *Come, let us return to the Lord, for it is He who has torn us to pieces, but He will heal us; He has struck us, but He will bind our wounds. He will revive us after two days; on the third day He will raise us up, to live in His presence. Let us know, let us strive to know the Lord; as certain as the dawn is His coming, His judgement shines forth like the light of day! He will come to us like the rain, like spring rain that waters the earth. "What can I do with you, Ephraim? What can I do with you, Judah? Your love is like a morning cloud, like the dew that early passes away. For this reason I smote them through the prophets, I slew them by the words of my mouth; for it is love that I desire, not sacrifice, and knowledge of God rather than holocausts"* (*Hos.* 6:1-6).

*　　*　　*　　*　　*　　*　　*

I AM GIVING YOU JESUS with LOVE

Dear Children! Rejoice with me! My heart is rejoicing because of Jesus and today I want to give Him to you. Dear children, I want each one of you to open your heart to Jesus and I will give Him to you with love. Dear children, I want Him to change you, to teach you and to protect you. Today I am praying in a special way for each one of you and I am presenting you to God so He will manifest Himself in you. I am calling you to sincere prayer with the heart so that every prayer of yours may be an encounter with God. In your work and in your everyday life, put God in the first place. I call you today with great seriousness to obey me and to do as I am calling you. Thank you for having responded to my call (December 25, 1987).

It is Christmas. Joy is in every heart. This is a feast when hearts open easier to God and to people. Warm hearts become even warmer, and many cold hearts become warm. God comes among His people as a child from a simple mother. This is the reason for a change in conduct of people which sometimes, unfortunately, is very short-lived. Mary prays that God will manifest Himself in us and that we will receive Him with love as she is offering Him. This is not hard at Christmas-time when it is easier to pray with joy, and prayer really becomes a meeting with God.

However, Christmas comes only once a year. Therefore, Mary calls us to put God in the first place every day of our lives. This means that we should renounce everything that is in the way in our daily life so that God can be in the first place in our thoughts, words, and deeds. God is approachable because He came as a child. He is understandable, because He is simple and acceptable and because He accepts. God becomes life; the way, the truth, and the light. For that reason we need to decide for Him with great joy and seriousness, and we listen to Him.

Our Lady invites us to joy. The basis for her human joy is the presence of Jesus Christ to Whom she opened her heart with love. She knows the conditions for joy. Therefore, she calls us to open ourselves. Mary accepted Jesus as a gift from God. God gave Himself to her with love so that she would experience His fullness. Mary offers Jesus to us with the desire that our acceptance of Him will enrich our lives, just as her life was enriched.

Whoever receives God does not receive Him because he is good, but he receives God in order to become good. God does not wait for us to change our lives, but comes as soon as we open ourselves, in order to help us change our lives. He does not come because we know all things, but rather to teach and guide us. Whoever allows himself to be led and taught will find himself in a most beautiful school. He will receive deep wisdom and the most beautiful of gifts, love. The brevity of Christian joy is caused by the path on which a person walks. On this path, evil hinders our walk with God, Who became our companion on this path and in our suffering. Mary becomes such a companion as well. At Christmas, we come out richer in the most beautiful company offered to man, Jesus and Mary. To begin the journey with them means to be on the way of love and peace.

Now there were shepherds in that region living in the fields and keeping the night watch over their flock. The angel of the Lord appeared to them and the glory of the Lord shone around them, and they were struck with great fear. The angel said to them, "Do not be afraid; for behold, I proclaim to you good news of great joy that will be for all the people. For today in the city of David a savior has been born for you who is Messiah and Lord. And this will be a sign for you: you will find an infant wrapped in swaddling clothes and lying in a manger." And suddenly there was a multitude of the heavenly host with the angel, praising God and saying: "Glory to God in the highest and on earth peace to those on whom His favor rests" (Lk. 2:8-15).

LOVE POINTS the WAY to PEACE and SALVATION

Dear Children! Today again I am calling you to prayer and complete surrender to God. You know that I love you and am coming here out of love, so I could show you the path of peace and salvation for your souls. I want you to obey me and not permit Satan to seduce you. Dear children, Satan is very strong and, therefore, I ask you to dedicate your prayers to me so that those who are under his influence may be saved. Give witness by your life, sacrifice your lives for the salvation of the world. I am with you and I am grateful to you, and in heaven you shall receive the Father's reward which He has promised you. Therefore, little children, do not be afraid. If you pray, Satan cannot injure you even a little, because you are God's children and He is watching over you. Pray, and let the rosary always be in your hands as a sign to Satan that you belong to me. Thank you for having responded to my call (February 25, 1988).

Many people in today's world are walking the way of unrest, looking for peace but becoming even more unpeaceful. Desiring salvation, they walk farther from it. The further away we are from peace and salvation, the more anxious we become. The more anxious we are, the easier we lose the way and, instead of peace and salvation, unrest and damnation increase. God does not want us to destroy ourselves in this way. His will is our peace and our salvation because He knows that He is peace to our soul and He is life for us. He is the way for the one who is lost, the light for the one in darkness, joy to the one who mourns, and He is calling all of us.

In these times God is sending Mary and calling us through her. She constantly emphasizes that she comes with love and, with love, she is showing us the way to peace and salvation. She introduces herself as a leader and educator of her children.

There is a spiritual war all around us and Satan is strong. He deceives, makes war, destroys, and blinds us. So many have become victims of his action. In spite of that, we should not be afraid. Mary, Mother and leader, is being victorious with her own over Satan and his action. Total abandonment, acceptance of God's will, interior and exterior order, and obedience are the conditions for the triumph over Satan. With prayer as the most powerful means and the rosary as an outer sign, victory and reward will not be absent. Heaven is waiting for us. To start out with Mary, the Morning Star, is to start on the way of peace and salvation which conquers all evil.

Finally, draw your strength from the Lord and from His mighty power. Put on the armor of God so that you may be able to stand firm against the tactics of the devil. For our struggle is not with flesh and blood but with the principalities, with the powers, with the world rulers of this present darkness, with the evil spirits in the heavens. Therefore, put on the armor of God, that you may be able to resist on the evil day and, having done everything, to hold your ground. So stand fast with your loins girded in truth, clothed with righteousness as a breastplate, and your feet shod in readiness for the gospel of peace. In all circumstances, hold faith as a shield, to quench all flaming arrows of the evil one (Eph. 6:10-16).

*   *   *   *   *   *   *

TO OVERCOME the TEMPORAL with LOVE

Dear Children! Today also I am calling you to a complete surrender to God. You, dear children, are not conscious of how God loves you with such a great love. Because of it He permits me to be with you so I can instruct you and help you to find the way of peace. That way, however, you cannot discover if you do not pray. Therefore, dear children, forsake everything and consecrate your time to God and then God will bestow gifts upon you and bless you. Little children, do not forget that your life is fleeting like the spring flower which today is wondrously beautiful, but tomorrow has vanished. Therefore, pray in such a way that your prayer, your surrender to God may become like a road sign. That way your witness will not only have value for yourselves, but for all of eternity. Thank you for having responded to my call (March 25, 1988).

Love is recognized by the interest in the loved person. No one can say that he loves someone or something if he does not show an interest in the object of his love. Such is the case with the love of God. The God of our Fathers, the God of Jacob, the God of Joseph, the God of Abraham and Isaac is not the God who wants to remain alone in His happiness and peace. He does not want to sit on His throne, removing Himself from the fate of His people, His children whom He loves so much.

God loves man. But, the problem is not if man knows how much God loves him. It is not important for a mother that her child really knows what motherly love is, nor is this knowledge necessary for the development of a child. The problem is created when man rejects God's love and takes another love instead.

God's love is especially active in Mary, the Queen of Peace. When she teaches, guides, and reminds us, she does so with divine love. She does the same when she helps, promises, and blesses and when she is giving concrete advice. Her help is necessary to us for the present, for the future, and for eternity. Therefore, she invites us to consecrate our time to God. She reminds us so that our life is like a flower, telling us about the temporal so that we will not attach ourselves to anything in this world that could prevent our way to eternity.

With love, time also becomes both relatively short and eternal, because in love we really meet the temporal which does not scare us, and eternity which we look forward to. The present and future meet with love. Love transcends man into new space and time. Whoever lives in this way becomes free in this world and a witness and signpost to others for the present time and for eternity.

> *The brother in lowly circumstances should take pride in his high standing, and the rich one in his lowliness, for he will pass away "like the flower of the field." For the sun comes up with its scorching heat and dries up the grass, its flower droops, and the beauty of its appearance vanishes. So will the rich person fade away in the midst of his pursuits. Blessed is the man who perseveres in temptation, for when he has been proved he will receive the crown of life that He promised to those who love Him (Jas. 1:9-12).*

* * * * * * *

WITH LOVE to ENCOMPASS EVERYTHING

> *Dear Children! I am calling you to a complete surrender to God. Pray, little children, that Satan does not sway you like branches in the wind. Be strong in God. I desire that through you the whole world may get to know the God of joy. Neither be anxious nor worried. God will help you and*

show you the way. I want you to love all men with my love, both the good and the bad. Only that way will love conquer the world. Little children, you are mine. I love you and I want you to surrender to me so I can lead you to God. Pray without ceasing so that Satan cannot take advantage of you. Pray so that you realize that you are mine. I bless you with the blessing of joy. Thank you for having responded to my call (May 25, 1988).

If we ask ourselves again what love is and try to find an answer, we will see that there are many different answers. All the answers can be summarized in three different words. *Eros* is a physical love which is always advantageous. *Eros* seeks persons and things for personal enjoyment and uses others. *Fila* is a friendly love, but it is conditional. It gives as much as it wants to receive. If it does not receive then it is questionable. It is limited. *Agape* is a kind of love which has its foundation in God. It distributes itself without conditions. It rejoices when it can give of itself. That is really a eucharistic love which knows no boundaries and does not accept boundaries. The good ones are not its purpose nor are the evil ones its limit. It does not know national or religious boundaries. Man and woman do not exist for it, neither do the beautiful nor the ugly. For *Agape* love there exists only people and situations in which it can distribute itself and make them happy. In making others happy it realizes itself. This is true eucharistic love which becomes the way to peace and which embraces everyone. That is the love which is not proud, is not jealous, does not elevate itself, but rather serves.

To this kind of love Our Lady is leading us. It is the love which heals us from anxiety and worry, which selects the right moment and believes in a new day in which it will fulfill God's will. This is the love which Satan attacks the most and wants to divert us from. His goal is to prevent us from experiencing *Agape* love and return us to *Fila* and *Eros* love.

We cannot renounce these levels of love but they can lead to great deceit in the life of a Christian. Individuals and groups, religious communities, national entities, and also church parishes often remain on the level of *Fila* love. Closed in their own circles, they reject and judge others. They argue who has the truth and who sins against love and regard themselves as righteous. In this way, boundaries unfortunately become an excuse not to love instead of becoming proof of our need for unconditional eucharistic love. To pray and to know that God loves us, that Our Lady accepts us as her own, means to be on the way of true eucharistic, all embracing *Agape* love.

> *For those who live according to the flesh are concerned with the things of the flesh, but those who live according to the spirit with the things of the spirit. The concern of the flesh is death, but the concern of the spirit is life and peace. For the concern of the flesh is hostility toward God; it does not submit to the law of God, nor can it; and those who are in the flesh cannot please God. But you are not in the flesh; on the contrary, you are in the spirit, if only the Spirit of God dwells in you* (Rom. 8:5-9).

* * * * * * *

OUR DESIRES and GOD'S LOVE

Dear Children! Today I am calling you to the love which is loyal and pleasing to God. Little children, love bears everything bitter and difficult for the sake of Jesus Who is love. Therefore, dear children, pray God to come to your aid, not, however, according to your desires but according to His love. Surrender yourselves to God so that He may heal you, console you, and forgive everything inside you which is a hindrance on the way of love. In this way God can mold your life and you will grow in love. Dear children, glorify God with canticles of love so that God's love may be able to grow in you day by day to its fullness. Thank you for having responded to my call (June 25, 1988).

Prayer will be a meeting with God when we pray with the heart, with love. If prayer remains only conditional, if it is self-centered, then it is not a meeting with God on the level of *Agape* love, but on the level of *Fila.* Whenever our needs or the needs of others inspire us to prayer in order to ask something of God, there is danger of our not meeting the God of love. For we may not be looking for Him because He loves us, but rather because He can help us. It means we are in danger of creating an image of God according to our needs and so we distance ourselves from God as He really is.

For example, if we are sick, we look for a God Who heals. If we are poor, we seek the God Who can make us rich. If we are weak, we look for God Who is strong. If we are in sin, we look for a God Who is merciful. True, the God we believe in is rich, can heal, is almighty, and is merciful. However, it is not worthy of His love to look for Him only when we need Him.

Mary teaches us a correct practice of prayer. We need to look for God because He loves us. We need to approach Him out of thankfulness because He created us. Open and good love toward God is love which overcomes all of our needs and looks for God only because He is love. Mary knows that we need God's love the most and everything else will be given to us besides. Then we will experience consolation, help, and healing. First we receive what we need for our eternal salvation and then for our physical being.

We, however, have to realize that growing in love is most necessary for our spiritual, mental, and physical health. And love, without love, cannot grow. Fullness of human love is not measured by human measure, but rather with a divine measure, because its seed is divine and the conditions under which it can grow are also divine. With such love, bitterness and hardships are transformed and we are a step closer to the realization of the deepest desire in us to be like God.

> *As the hind longs for the running waters, so my*
> *   soul longs for you, O God.*
> *A thirst is my soul for God, the living God. When*
> *   shall I go and behold the face of God?*
> *My tears are my food day and night, as they say*

to me day after day, "Where is your God?"
Those times I recall, now that I pour out my soul
within me,
When I went with the throng and led them in
procession to the house of God,
Amid loud cries of joy and thanksgiving, with the
multitude keeping festival.
Why are you so downcast, O my soul?
Why do you sigh within me? Hope in God!
For I shall again be thanking Him, in the presence
of my Savior and my God

(Ps. 42:1-6).

*   *   *   *   *   *   *

DISCOVER JOY and LOVE

Dear Children! I am calling you to openness to God. You see, little children, how nature is opening herself and is giving life and fruits. In the same way I am calling you to a life with God and a complete surrender to Him. Little children, I am with you unceasingly and I desire to lead you into the joy of life. I desire that each one of you discovers the joy and the love which is found only in God and which only God can give. God wants nothing else from you but your surrender. Therefore, little children, decide seriously for God, because everything else passes away. God alone does not pass away. Pray that you may discover the greatness and the joy of life which God is giving you. Thank you for having responded to my call (May 25, 1989).

God is the fullness of non-temporal life. He is the fullness of love and joy. Man is created so that he needs joy and love as his daily bread. Therefore, man as a creature, yearns for a lasting life which death cannot endanger. However, the situation in which man finds himself in this world may seem hopeless. The chains of death are impenetrable and anxiety moves easily into his heart because his deepest desires are endangered, especially his life.

Whatever a man tries to hold on to in this world can slip away from his hands, and wherever he places his hopes seems to slip away from under his feet. Our lives as God's creatures are not prosperous when we simply isolate ourselves in this world of materialism.

Mary knows our situation. She lived in this world. She found true support in God and she knows the way which leads to the realization of life in love and joy. That way cannot be endangered even by death for the foundation of life is God. The word *Amen* which we so often use at the end of prayers has its roots in a Hebrew word which means steadfast, stand strong, to be near the spring of life and not be in danger (picture a mother with a child). When man is in God he stands so strong that even death leads him to life. The everlasting God is indeed assurance in this passing and crumbling world for our eternity. He wants us to run to His lap as a child runs to its parent's lap.

This message was given in May, when nature is awakening from its winter's sleep and dormant stage to a new life. Nature wakes up in such a way that it even brings fruit for the life of others. The sun is necessary, however. Whatever does not open to the sun, dies out and does not bring forth fruit. The beauty of nature in blossom can give encouragement to us and help us to open up to love and joy, because God is the one who renews. Life is a great gift of an alive God to Whom we should give thanks, honor, and glory.

Sing joyfully to God our strength; acclaim the God
of Jacob.
Take up a melody, and sound the timbrel, the
pleasant harp, and the lyre.
Blow the trumpet at the new moon, at the full
moon on our solemn feast.
I relieved his shoulder of the burden; his hands
were freed from the basket.
In distress you called, and I rescued you; unseen,
I answered you in thunder;
I tested you at the waters of Meribah.

Hear, my people, and I will admonish you; O Israel, will you not hear me?
There shall be no strange god among you, nor shall you worship any alien god.
I, the Lord, am your God, Who led you forth from the land of Egypt;
Open wide your mouth, and I will fill it...While Israel I would feed with the best of wheat, and with honey from the rock I would fill them
                                    (Ps. 81:1-4, 7-11, 17).

* * * * * * *

TIME of GRACE

Dear Children! Today I call you to live the messages which I have been giving you during the past eight years. This is the time of grace and I desire the grace of God be great for every single one of you. I am blessing you and I love you with a special love. Thank you for having responded to my call (June 25, 1989).

Eight years have passed since the beginning of the apparitions. This is the length of grade school. Time is precious, especially because Mary, the teacher and Mother of Life, is with us. This is the time of grace. Her wish and mission is to be with us and to help us so that we enter into grace. To be in grace means to be in complete unity with God and with one another. This is another expression for peace. Therefore, Our Lady desires that the grace of God be great for each one of us. Grace is ready and waits for us. We simply need to open ourselves and it will flow in like a river because Christ earned it for all of us, and Mary intercedes constantly for it for us.

Mary gives blessings. She does this especially on her feast days and special occasions, such as the eighth anniversary of her apparitions when she gave the above message. A

95

blessing has deep meaning. The Latin expression *benedicere* means to speak well, to wish well, to think well and so create and radiate good. Mary blesses. That means that she intercedes for us and she speaks for us before God.

In her intercession for us, she manifests her love. She is the Woman clothed with sun, with stars around her head and a moon under her feet and she fights against Satan. Satan's role is to judge, to condemn, to speak evil, to destroy, and to take joy in damnation. Everything that Our Lady wants to teach us in everyday life we can express in the word *blessing*. But as for us, love is necessary for us to be able to bless ourselves and others, God and nature. To bless our families, our communities, the Church, and our nation means to intercede with love for others and to create healthy relationships which bring light, peace, hope, and joy.

To begin the ninth year of apparitions with a blessing means we are off to a good beginning and good continuation of Our Lady's work. It means we have an assurance to continue willingly to live and to work.

> *The Lord bless you and keep you! The Lord let His face shine upon you, and be gracious to you! The Lord look upon you kindly and give you peace (Nm. 6:24-26).*

*   *   *   *   *   *   *

I LOVE YOU and I WANT to LEAD YOU on the WAY of PEACE

> *Dear Children! Today I invite you to peace. I have come here as the Queen of Peace and I desire to enrich you with my motherly peace. Dear Children, I love you and I desire to bring all of you to the peace which only God gives and which enriches every heart. I invite you to become carriers and witnesses of my peace to this unpeaceful world. Let peace rule in the whole world which is without peace and longs for peace. I bless you*

with my motherly blessing. Thank you for having responded to my call (July 25, 1990).

In order to understand this message it is necessary to call to mind world events at the time the message was given. It was just before Iraq's attack on Kuwait, a situation which caused great tension and a real crisis in the world. Several months later, in January 1991, the war began. At the same time the tension in Croatia was growing. Many people thought, some even were deeply convinced, that war was impossible. War, a real terrible war, happened nevertheless in Kuwait, in Croatia, and in Bosnia-Hercegovina. No war in the world has been worse in killing, destruction, and hatred than the war in Bosnia-Hercegovina. Many human victims fell, the innocent suffered. Many churches and shrines were destroyed or desecrated. Hospitals, schools, and family homes were destroyed. All this happened because an army attacked an unarmed people, destroying everything that belonged to the people and occupying territory that belonged to others.

Mary loves us and calls us to peace. She calls us to prayer and fasting for peace. She wants to enrich us with her motherly peace and make us witnesses of peace. The world yearns for peace, but it is helpless to create conditions for peace. Our Lady offers her motherly blessing, and that means, as a mother, she wants to protect us from destruction. No one can love life more than a mother does. Therefore, no one can desire to protect life like a mother. All people are her children and she wants peace for all. Peace really is a call to decide with love to guard and honor life. Whoever decides for life, decides for God, Who wants to enrich us with His peace today, tomorrow, every day, and for all eternity. The goal is accepted, the way exists. We only need to start!

> *I will hear what God proclaims; the Lord, for He
>   proclaims peace.*
> *To His people, and to His faithful ones, and to
>   those who put in Him their hope.*
> *Near indeed is His salvation to those who fear*

Him, glory dwelling in our land.
Kindness and truth shall meet; justice and peace
   shall kiss.
Truth shall spring out of the earth, and justice
   shall look down from Heaven.
The Lord Himself will give His benefits; Our land
   shall yield its increase.
Justice shall walk before Him, and salvation,
   along the way of His steps

                                        (*Ps.* 85:9-14)

*   *   *   *   *   *   *

WITH LOVE and OUT of LOVE

Dear Children! Today I invite you to do works
of mercy with love, and out of love for me and
for your and my brothers and sisters. Dear chil-
dren, all that you do for others, do it with great
joy and humility towards God. I am with you and
day after day I offer you sacrifices and prayers to
God for the salvation of the world. Thank you for
having responded to my call (November 25, 1990).

The main rule of life for Christ's disciples is to love with
merciful love. This is one of the most concrete ways Christ
recognizes His disciples and gives life in eternal, merciful,
divine love. However, He, through His merciful love, will not
recognize those who have called His name or preached in
His name without giving mercy and without love.

Mary teaches us how we should perform acts of mercy.
It is obvious that doing something is not enough but how
we do it is important. Whatever we do for others we should
do with love and out of love. Acts of help which are not
done with love and out of love can be degrading for the one
who receives them and they only feed the conceit and pride
of those who performed them.

To humbly do the deeds of mercy means that we understand that whatever we have, we have received from God.

98

All that we have that is not necessary to us, we should place at the disposal of our brothers and sisters who are in need. Mary is encouraging us to perform deeds with love and thanking God so that selfishness would not change the divine rule and find an excuse for not performing according to God's commandments.

Of course, we cannot neglect the expression from the message, "your and my brothers and sisters." Mary is not only our mother and teacher, intercessor and guide, but she is also a sister to all of us. She is our mother, because Jesus from the Cross gave us to her and asked her to receive us as her children. She is our teacher because she teaches us to pray and to live in faith. And she is our sister because she calls God her Father for she is His most favored daughter and handmaid.

Finally, whatever we do should not only be done with love and in love, but also with joy. Joy is born at the moment a person knows that his deeds and words are in accord with the inner voice of his conscience and so according to God's will.

We always give thanks to God, the Father of Our Lord Jesus Christ, when we pray for you, for we have heard of your faith in Christ Jesus and the love that you have for all the holy ones because of the hope reserved for you in Heaven. Of this you have already heard through the word of truth, the gospel, that has come to you. Just as in the whole world it is bearing fruit and growing, so also among you, from the day you heard it and came to know the grace of God in truth... (Col. 1:3-5).

*   *   *   *   *   *   *

TO RENEW LOVE TOWARD JESUS

Dear Children! Again today I invite you to live the passion of Jesus in prayer and in union with Him. Decide to give more time to God, who gave you these days of grace. Therefore, dear children, pray and in a special way renew your love for Jesus in your heart. I am with you and I accompany you with my blessing and my prayers. Thank you for having responded to my call (March 25, 1991).

This message was given in Lent. Lent is a time when we remember Christ's love and what He suffered for us. It provides us with an opportunity to understand how suffering by itself did not bring and earn salvation, but the love with which Christ endured His passion and His cross accomplished our salvation. Helpful acts for others become acts of mercy only when we do them with joy, humbly, and with love and out of love. In the same way, the question of our crosses becomes redemptive suffering when we carry them with love. Christ's reminding the women of Jerusalem not to cry for Him but for themselves and their children who need conversion is a reminder to all of us.

We do not celebrate Lent nor do we remember Christ's passion so that we can cry about what He suffered, but we do so in order to renew our love toward Him. We celebrate Lent in order to receive new encouragement to grow in love, so that we can carry our crosses and our burdens with love. Without love they will not have the value for eternity which they should have, and that would be a real loss.

Mary knows human life and she wants to educate us. She knows that through suffering, friendships are made and love matures. She knows that by looking at Christ we can grow in love of Him and grow in that Love which carries the crosses and makes the sacrifices and transforms them into good for us and for the glory of God. To observe Christ's love in suffering, to enter into the mystery of that love, means to become able to live the life worthy of man. To think and to meditate, to meet and to be with Christ Who suffers means to discover true love and constantly grow in it. The price for mature, perfect love is suffering. Through love suffering becomes easier because the one who loves can also suffer. On the tree of suffering love is the most beautiful fruit.

He grew up like a sapling before him, like a shoot from the parched earth; there was in him no stately bearing to make us look at him, nor appearance that would attract us to him. He was spurned and avoided by men, a man of suffering, accustomed to infirmity, one of those from whom men hide their faces, spurned, and we held him in no esteem. Yet it was our infirmities that he bore, our sufferings that he endured, while we thought of him as stricken, as one smitten by God and afflicted. But he was pierced for our offenses, crushed for our sins, upon him was the chastisement that makes us whole, by his stripes we were healed... Because of his affliction we shall see the light in fullness of days through his suffering, my servant shall justify many, and their guilt he shall bear. Therefore I will give him his portion among the great, and he shall divide the spoils with the mighty, because he surrendered himself to death and was counted among the wicked; and he shall take away the sins of many, and win pardon for their offenses (*Is.* 53:2-5, 11-12).

* * * * * * *

SERIOUSNESS and LOVE

Dear Children! Today I invite all of you who have heard my message of peace to realize it with seriousness and with love in your life. There are many who think that they are doing a lot by talking about the messages, but they do not live them. Dear Children, I invite you to life and to change all the negative in you so that it all turns into the positive and life. Dear Children I am with you and I desire to help each of you to live and by living to witness the Good News. I am here, dear children, to help you and to lead you to Heaven, and in Heaven is the Joy through which you can already live Heaven now. Thank you for having responded to my call (May 25, 1991).

In order to understand this message which calls us to renew the message of peace with seriousness and love, we need to recall the situation and the events in the Croatian nation and other non-Serb nations. This message was given one month before war began in the former Yugoslavia. It began in Slovenia on June 26, 1991. It moved to Croatia shortly after and then on to Bosnia-Hercegovina. Even though Our Lady did not come to record war chronology, we can understand and interpret these events in the light of the messages.

We are witnesses of how much evil, hate, and revenge has accumulated in the hearts of people. Politics in former Yugoslavia intentionally deepened wounds and constantly opened new wounds (especially Serbia) so that one could easily feel the coming culmination, an awful war, in the same way as an accumulation of clouds produces a downpour of rain. Politicians from Serbia always talked about peace, but they were preparing for war. In Croatia, fear and insecurity were spreading and people would have to face the possibility of war against a well-armed army.

Mary as mother, follows the situation and shows us the best solution, to clean out all that is bad starting with ourselves. Then everyone will be able to experience joy in peace and ensure peace with joy. Spiritually conquering that which is bad would prevent war because war is the worst result of the hatred in human hearts. However, many remained deaf and mute to these calls of Our Mother and many did not understand the seriousness of the situation and they did not try to change it with love. And while Mary's call found many closed hearts, hate in its own action prepared for war and destruction. Evil was organizing itself better than the good was organizing. Active hatred is more effective than love and the spirit of revenge does not let it rest in peace. Mary calls for a change of life so that all the bad can be transformed to good and right. Change or conversion means freeing oneself from sin and its bad side effects, thus enabling us for good. It is again the way of joy and the way of peace.

When the war is over, this message will have even greater meaning not only for those who survived the war and are deeply hurt, but for all people who live in conflict, who do not forgive, who become dependent, or who lose hope. All these are the results of sin. If we are called to stop small wars and small destruction, then big wars will not be possible.

> *The eleven disciples went to Galilee, to the mountain to which Jesus had ordered them. Then they saw Him, they worshiped, but they doubted. Then Jesus approached and said to them, "All power in Heaven and on earth has been given to me. Go, therefore, and make disciples of all nations, baptizing them in the name of the Father, and of the Son, and of the Holy Spirit, teaching them to observe all that I have commanded you. And behold, I am with you always, until the end of the age." (Mt. 28:16-20).*

*   *   *   *   *   *   *

MAY YOUR HEART BE a SPRING of LOVE

> *Dear Children! This time, also, I am inviting you to prayer. Pray that you might be able to comprehend what God desires to tell you through my presence and through the messages I am giving you. I desire to draw you ever closer to Jesus and to His wounded heart, that you might be able to comprehend the immeasurable Love which gave itself for each one of you. Therefore, dear children, pray that from your heart would flow a fountain*

of love to every person both to the one who hates you and to the one who despises you. That way you will be able, through Jesus' love, to overcome all the misery in this world of sorrow, which is without hope for those who do not know Jesus. I am with you and I love you with the immeasurable love of Jesus. Thank you for all your sacrifices and prayers. Pray so I might be able to help you still more. Your prayers are necessary to me. Thank you for having responded to my call (November 25, 1991).

The cross of Christ is a sign of Christ's love. His wounded heart is, in a special way, a token of His suffering love. There are moments of suffering when a person cannot hear words of consolation, but only finds strength in the presence of dear friends or family. Those are the moments when even friends do not have strength to say, "It will be better," but remain silent and show their love by their silent presence.

This message was given at the time of enormous suffering in Eastern Slavonia (a province of Croatia), especially in the city of Vukovar. The city was totally destroyed. Thousands of people, women, children, the old, the weak, the sick were killed or taken as slaves to Serbian prisons. Croatian pride was deeply hurt. The Croatian soul was offended and Croatian eyes were crying at seeing the awful suffering and destruction of all that is Croatian. There was deep sorrow among those who remained. But, there was also fear and anxiety because the aggressor was threatening and in his aggression he realized his plans. The situation was indescribable and could not be put in human words.

In the message, Mary is especially gentle. She invites us to come closer to Christ's wounded heart, which loves us immeasurably. We need to come closer to His heart because we ourselves need to be healed first, and then our hearts will become the source of love, consolation, and hope for other people. Our Lady is inviting us to allow His love to flow from our hearts toward those who hate and despise us. Only with love can we overcome sorrow and sorrowful situations. Those who do not know Christ, the light and the life, are especially in a grave situation. Victory is insured through the love of Christ. It is of enormous importance that all of these suffering redemptions be presented to the Lord with love.

The time of war passes. The dead will be buried and mourned. Cities will be rebuilt, but history will go further. The value of this message will remain always because people will act in a human way. There will always be those who are degraded, castaway, and despised because there will always be those who hate, despise, and do evil. The best and most effective means to counter this is to be constantly close to Christ Who loves us and Who shows us the way through His own suffering. Our hearts will then be able to be new and become a source of love. This is Mary's wish.

> *Your holy cities have become a desert; Zion is a desert, Jerusalem a desolation. Our holy and glorious temple in which our fathers praised you has been burned with fire; all that was dear to us lies in ruins. Can you hold back, O Lord, after all this? Can you remain silent, and afflict us so severely? (Is. 64:10-11). So the soldiers came and broke the legs of the first and then of the other one who was crucified with Jesus. But when they came to Jesus and saw that He was already dead, they did not break His legs, but one soldier thrust his lance into His side, and immediately blood and water flowed out (Jn. 19:32-34).*

* * * * * * *

A BLESSING of PEACE and LOVE

> *Dear Children! Today in a special way, I bring the little Jesus to you that He may bless you with His blessings of peace and love. Dear Children, do not forget that this is a grace which many people neither understand nor accept. Therefore, you have said that you are mine and seek my help, give all of yourself. First of all, give your love and*

example in your families. You say that Christmas is a family feast. Therefore, dear children, put God in the first place in your families so that He may give you peace and may protect you not only from war but also protect you from every satanic attack during peace. When God is with you, you have everything. But when you do not want Him, then you are miserable and lost, and you do not know on whose side you are. Therefore, dear children, decide for God and then you will get everything. Thank you for having responded to my call (December 25, 1991).

Christmas is the time when we celebrate Mary's bringing Jesus Who gives blessings of love and peace. In days of war, nothing is more needed than the blessing of peace and love. Peace is needed more than health, or family home, or freedom. To be without the blessing of peace and love means to be blind to that which we have, and to be unhappy in that which we have, and this is worse than not to have. There are so many people in the world who are healthy and have everything, but they have lost their peace and they are not able to love. They suffer much, destroying their life and the lives of others. The blessing of peace and love has its conditions, however. God must be in the first place, not only in individual hearts, but in families and in communities. When God takes first place, then all hearts will experience the blessing of love and peace.

War is an awful thing. It is in the time of darkness that we understand better just how much we need the light! It is in the time of hatred that we understand that we need love. It is in the time of destruction that we come to understand how our life is passing and how the work of our hands is exposed to termination! War is also a time when we come to the realization of how much we need protection!

However, the time after war is not easy either. Hearts are in danger of remaining closed for a long time by hatred. The spirit of revenge can creep in. Sorrow and despair can overwhelm those who are left without their dear ones. Satan wants to use this situation and deceive hearts for evil.

106

However, those times when the war is far away are not safe from these same attacks. True protection rests in our opening up to God and allowing God to protect us.

In this message we again discover what is most important that Mary wants to teach us. God is everything to us. Without Him we are miserable and in darkness, unprotected and open to every destructive power, whether it comes from our own selves or from others. Mary calls us to decide for God, consciously and responsibly. This is the first step on the way to salvation. God took this step in Jesus. What remains is that each one of us gives an answer. To know on which side we are means to know the way through life and the purpose of life. God started to walk with us and all will be all right if we allow Him not only to sojourn with us, but also to lead us.

I give thanks to my God always on your account for the grace of God bestowed on you in Christ Jesus, that in Him you were enriched in every way, with all discourse and all knowledge, as the testimony to Christ was confirmed among you. So you are not lacking in any spiritual gift as you wait for the revelation of Our Lord Jesus Christ. He will keep you firm to the end, irreproachable on the day of Our Lord Jesus. God is faithful and by Him you were called to fellowship with His Son, Jesus Christ Our Lord (1 Cor. 1:4-9).

*   *   *   *   *   *   *

OASIS of PEACE, GOODNESS, and LOVE

Dear Children! Today, as never before, I invite you to live my messages and to put them into practice in your life. I have come to you to help you and therefore, I invite you to change your life because you have taken a path of misery, a path of ruin. When I told you, "Convert, pray, fast, be reconciled," you took these messages superficially.

You started to live them and then you stopped because it was difficult for you. Know, dear children, when something is good you have to persevere in the good and not think, "God does not see me. He is not with me. He is not helping." And so, you have gone away from God and from me because of your miserable interests. I wanted to create of you an oasis of peace, love, and goodness. God wanted you, with your love and with His help, to do miracles and thus give an example. Therefore, here is what I say to you: Satan is playing with you and with your souls and I cannot help you because you are far away from my heart. Therefore, pray, live my messages, and then you will see the miracles of God's love in your everyday life. Thank you for having responded to my call (March 25, 1992).

In the first eleven years of her apparitions, Our Lady mentioned the word *love* sixty-two times. We meditated on her messages. Closing the circle of our meditations before the eleventh anniversary and just before war began in Bosnia-Hercegovina, this message echoed in the hearts of many as a reprimand, as objection. It seems that Our Lady, carrying her flag in front of us for eleven years, encouraging us to peace and love, lowered this flag at half-staff. She objects to our superficial way in living the messages and that we do not have enough perseverance. And then we complain, accusing God Who does not see and does not hear, and Who does not help us. The word that she wanted to create with us, an oasis of peace and love, echoed within us and we were on the way to ruin. This is the opposite way of peace. It is a direction which Satan advises. In this situation, because we are free, God becomes helpless, and Mary cannot help us either. The first step is up to us. To accept the messages means to allow God to perform miracles again.

The war came. It is awful and terrible. Many victims have fallen, many homes and churches have been burned. There has been much suffering, deep sorrow, anxiety, and wounds in soul and body. Now the question arises. Could we have, based on conversion, fasting, and prayer, avoided this war and all that happened? Some are convinced that the war is punishment because we did not listen to the voice of God. It is impossible to answer this question. But the fact is that this war was announced ten years ago, when the apparitions started on June 25, 1981. Then, Our Lady cried and invited us to prayer and fasting, to stop wars. No war yet has generated as much prayer as this one. People all over the world have been praying. The parish community has taken part in it. This war is not the response to our prayers and fasting; but peace, which is to come, will be a great gift.

The situation could be much different if everyone accepted God's call. For even if many people have not believed that Our Lady comes here to Medjugorje, they could have realized that we need peace and that we can pray for it. While we mourn for all victims, crying for them, the hope still remains that we will come out of this situation more able to live in peace. With this hope, I hand over this booklet and again I express my wish that it will awaken in every person a deep desire for love and that everyone will open up like a spring flower to the action of God's love. Peace will come. It will meet with justice and embrace in every family, church, and the world. These are Mary's times. Through her, the Queen of Peace and the Queen of Prophets, God will continue to act. Everyone can become the oasis of peace, goodness, and love which Mary speaks about. May it be so!

May the Lord, the spring of Peace Himself give you peace at all times and in every way. May the Lord be with all of you (2 Thes. 3:16).

*   *   *   *   *   *   *

IN PLACE of CONCLUSION

I wrote this booklet at the time of war. Listening daily about hatred, about the spirit of revenge, about destructions, killings, and imprisonments, I would sometimes lose courage and the willingness to go on with this booklet. It is not easy to write about love when hate is in action. And it is even harder then, to live and practice love. Therefore, I decided every day to pray for myself and for all people, to be worthy to receive love, and to be able to spread love.

Meditating and writing these lines, I became sad and at the same time again joyful. From day to day I realized how all of us are far from love, and for that reason we are anxious, unhappy, and destroyed. This made me sad. Joy came again because I feel that it is indeed possible to begin on the way of love and peace in spite of everything. For this is the will of God for us and He offers us His help. Therefore, I decided to seek His help daily and every day to try to overcome our limitations of love and so free love from human chains, for everything is possible with God in our life.

Now I am even more thankful to Mary, Mother of Love, that she has stayed with us so long. One of the reasons for her staying was to teach us to love. Therefore, I invite all people, in the name of the Mother of Love, to open themselves, without any fear, to her Motherly love. Then we will be preserved in peace and one day we will receive the gift of eternal peace in the God of love.

Faith Publishing Company

Faith Publishing Company has been organized as a service for the publishing and distribution of materials that reflect Christian values, and in particular the teachings of the Catholic Church.

It is dedicated to publication of only those materials that reflect such values.

Faith Publishing Company also publishes books for The Riehle Foundation. The Foundation is a non-profit, tax-exempt producer and distributor of Catholic books and materials worldwide, and also supplies hospital and prison ministries, churches and mission organizations.

For more information on the publications of Faith Publishing Company, contact:

Faith Publishing Company
P.O. BOX 237
MILFORD, OHIO 45150

Books published by Faith Publishing Company can be ordered as follows:

Individuals send
requests to:

The Riehle Foundation
P.O. Box 7
Milford, Ohio 45150
513-576-0032

Book stores and
centers, contact:

Faith Publishing Company
P.O. Box 237
Milford, Ohio 45150
513-576-6400
513-576-0022 (Fax)

Canadian
Distributor:

B. Broughton Company Limited
2105 Danforth Ave.
Toronto, Ontario
Canada M4C 1K1
416-690-4777
416-690-5357 (Fax)